Questioning Strategies
and Techniques

Questioning Strategies and Techniques

Francis P. Hunkins
University of Washington

ALLYN AND BACON, INC., BOSTON

Printed in the United States of America
Library of Congress Catalog Card Number: 70–177289

To my wife, Doreen

Contents

Preface

Exciting events are taking place today in both curriculum and instruction. New curriculum projects have great potential for stimulating students, and many new instructional strategies are being developed to involve students more actively in their learning. However, research conducted by myself and others indicates that much of our questioning behavior is not as effective or as productive as we had thought. It also became evident that there is a lack of sufficient material available to teachers who want help in formulating creative questioning strategies. This book is intended to provide teachers as well as students with the tools for increasing their skills in effective question-asking. It is organized not only to give the reader a keen insight into the relevance of the questioning process to education today, but also to give him a good working knowledge of inductive strategies and how to apply them to his particular program. Chapter 1 discusses the vital importance of questions to the discovery curriculum and the current educational scene. Chapter 2 presents an abbreviated outline of Bloom's Taxonomy and gives examples of types of questions directed at each level. Guidelines for developing effective questions are presented in Chapter 3. Also this chapter makes the student aware of the questioning process as a tool for his own use. Chapter 4 goes on to present a variety of questioning strategies designed to achieve different results. Chapter 5 offers the reader different methods for evaluating the effectiveness of his and his students' question-asking behaviors. Finally,

Chapter 6 discusses the effects that using the questioning strategies will have on both the teacher and the student and promotes an attitude of inquiry.

The book combines practical guidelines for forming questions designed to improve student interest and includes the major thinking of such contemporary authorities as Bloom, Suchman, and Taba. It is a vital reference for educators at all levels—elementary, secondary, college, and in-service teacher training.

I extend my appreciation and thanks to those publishers who allowed me to quote or paraphrase selections from their books, as well as to John D. Peters, editor at Allyn and Bacon, for his encouragement and assistance during the preparation of the manuscript. I also wish to indicate my appreciation to Dr. A. Lawrence Gagnon, Superintendent of Schools, Hillsdale Community Schools, Hillsdale, Michigan, and to Dr. Drew Tinsley, Associate Professor of Education, Texas A & I University, Laredo, who reviewed the text. My family, especially my wife, Doreen, who served as typist, proofreader, idea reactor, and moral support during the entire time of manuscript preparation, deserve special thanks. My children, Leah and Francis, Jr., allowed their father to spend many uninterrupted hours at the typewriter, for which I thank them.

Francis P. Hunkins

Questioning Strategies
and Techniques

1

New Emphasis in a New Dimension

The question is central to learning. For over two thousand years since the Greek philosopher Socrates used a method of questioning to arrive at a definition, the question has been a part of teaching. Yet only within the last decade and a half has extensive research been directed to questions and questioning strategies. Information from this research indicates that teachers largely have been asking the wrong questions. We have primarily been asking questions regarding the specific information students possessed rather than questions to promote learning.

EMPHASIS UPON PROCESS

In the fifties a greater emphasis was placed on the disciplines and on the various methodologies unique to the disciplines. With this stress on the disciplines, educators were urged to allow their students opportunities to employ these processes of investigation. The question is common to the various scientific strategies or processes. Individuals ask questions to identify the reason or reasons for search. Individuals ask questions to direct their search and to synthesize information. Individuals ask questions to evaluate conclusions resulting from investigation. Questions are used in scientific investigation to provide additional information and guide in achieving new insights. Using the question to assist one's investigation is a new use of the question in the schools. In the past, teachers primarily questioned to ascertain if students were learning book content and to check if students were attending.

Some have attributed the shift of emphasis from learning solely content to learning process to the launching of the Russian Sputnik in 1957. However, American educators were seeking ways to vitalize American schooling in the early 1950s. Part of this shift resulted from the natural evolution of educational thought. In the fifties various scholars were beginning to engage students in experiences more closely resembling those of scholars. Scholars were not passive receivers of information; they were active searchers.

By the early 1960s a number of curricular projects had emerged: PSSC Physics, BSCS, CHEM Study, AAAS, SMSG Math, and others.[1] The National Science Foundation had funded several of these projects. The projects emphasized not only content but process. The federal government's changing attitude, exemplified by supplying increased federal monies, also supported the shift to process learning. Effective education was necessary for national defense.

With such a shift of emphasis education assumed, at least partially, a new posture. Many educators no longer were content at having pupils learn history just by reading history texts. Historians analyzed numerous types of documents. To learn the historical approach, pupils also should function in a manner resembling that of the historian. Such functioning would enable pupils to gain an increased understanding of relationships among historical data. It also could develop more positive student attitudes toward the discipline. Similar aims existed for other disciplines. Pupils were to understand the modes of inquiry of the geographer, of the physicist, and of the

---

[1] The reader is advised to check in John I. Goodland et al., *The Changing Curriculum* (New York: Fund for the Advancement of Education, 1966) for a somewhat detailed account of some major curriculum projects.

mathematician in order to comprehend more completely the relationships within each of these realms of scholarship.

A prime reason for this shift of emphasis was and is to enable individuals to deal intelligently with their world, their lives. If students can analyze their lives and the lives of others while in the school setting, they will comprehend effectively their reality when outside the formal school situation. Education aims at the creation of a rational being.[2] A rational being is not merely one who possesses an effective memory. He must be able to react to data. He must be able to think; he must be active in seeking understanding. However, the stress on rationalism should not be at the expense of the individual's affective domain. Indeed, if one better understands various situations and phenomena, he has a better chance for being affectively tuned to his world. A person who comprehends the complexity of another culture certainly has a chance of developing more favorable attitudes toward that group than an individual who lacks such knowledge.

NEW GOALS

The emphasis on process shifted priorities. During the fifties attention shifted from teaching specific facts to ways of dealing with concepts and generalizations. The knowledge explosion itself exerts pressure for the change of focus. New information is now being generated at a rate faster than at any time previously. In the last decade man discovered more knowledge than he had acquired in the previous half century. Estimates indicate that almost two thousand years passed before man doubled his knowledge. Present estimates are that knowledge will double in periods of less than ten years!

This tremendous increase in the quantity of knowledge has, of course, increased the number of specific facts. To teach all these specific facts in school would be an impossible task, even if to attempt to do so were a sound idea. But specific

[2] National Education Association, *Schools for The Sixties* (New York: McGraw-Hill, 1963).

facts lack full meaning if they are not related to other facts and to other types of information.

Students require means and opportunities to comprehend how groups of specific facts interrelate. What are their common characteristics? Can this grouping of facts be organized further according to some commonality? Grouping of data is one way by which individuals can distinguish various data. This grouping allows one to react to data classes. Such reacting provides concept learning. Concept learning is one of the new goals for education.

Information can be grouped to form what have been called concrete concepts and abstract concepts.[3] *Concrete concepts* are learned from observation. The learner can see these concepts or at least the phenomena from which these concepts evolve; he can manipulate these concepts to study relationships. For example, "house" and "flower" are concrete concepts. The words apply to groupings of data or phenomena according to common characteristics. The learner has observed many structures and has identified such common characteristics as walls, windows, roofs, and doors. He has learned to recognize these phenomena to be of the class "house." All other structures that he encounters he can class as houses if they possess these basic common characteristics. In learning concepts, the learner is asking questions. He asks questions that direct his attention to significant elements and to relationships among those elements. The same is true with the concept "flower." The learner observes a plant and asks questions that enable him to discriminate among its parts. What parts does it have? What function does each part serve? What color does the blossom have? How long was it on the plant? Is it like anything else ever observed? Notice the questions. If a person has observed other flowers, he then records how this specific item resembles the previous flowers observed.

The *abstract concept* is the second type; this is the con-

---

[3] Robert M. Gagne, 2d ed., *The Conditions of Learning* (New York: Holt, Rinehart & Winston, 1970), p. 171.

cept by definition.[4] These concepts exhibit relationships. Individuals cannot learn these concepts by observation in the way they learn concrete concepts. Rather they must learn such concepts by definition, primarily through verbal means. These concepts also can be called relational concepts. Gagne in discussing these concepts gives "bottle cap" as an example of a defined concept. This concept indicates the relationship between the bottle and the closing of its top. It represents a composite of the concepts of "bottle," "top," and "close."

TEACHING CONCEPTS

Gagne clearly explains how one can teach a concrete concept. One wishes to teach a seven-year-old the concept "odd." Three hollow blocks are placed on the table. Two of the blocks are identical; the third block is different. The child is told that a small piece of candy has been placed under one of the blocks. The child engages in trial and error behavior to discover where the candy was placed. Several more situations are presented with the candy always being placed under the odd block, the different one. The child continues to discover where the candy is. Such discovery reinforces his idea that the candy will be under the odd or different block. Soon the child does not go through extensive trial and error but goes directly to the different block. The experimenter then brings in another set of blocks, two identical and one different. After a few attempts the child goes to the different block. Once the child finds the candy by this method without error he is using the concept "odd."[5]

Gagne[6] indicates that we do not know how many situations one needs to learn a concept. However, it is evident from the example that the child must be involved in his learning.

---

[4] Ibid., p. 171.

[5] Ibid., pp. 172-74. Adapted and reprinted by permission of Holt, Rinehart & Winston, Inc.

[6] Ibid., p. 176

But the child needs to encounter many situations of the concept in question in order to experience the range of situations in which the concept exists. If one wishes to teach the concept "middle," one would need to structure many situations in which something, was in the middle of something else. If one wishes a student to understand the concept "mountain," many situations would need to be presented for the student to discriminate between topographic features and conceptualize mountain.

INVOLVEMENT WITH KNOWLEDGE— PART OF THE NEW GOALS

In schools emphasizing the process approach, students don't just learn concepts; they use them. Once a certain concept is attained, the teacher provides students with opportunities to apply the concept to new situations. In such a way the student achieves a much broader base for dealing with his world. He is no longer limited to specific stimuli. He can deal with vast groupings of data and the relationships among such data.

Considering relationships among concepts involves dealing with generalizations. These statements of abstract ideas provide the student with information that he can apply to numerous situations. He can group a tremendous amount of data in such a statement. The generalization from anthropology that "the art, music, architecture, food, clothing, sports, and customs of a people help to produce a national identity" allows for the organization of vast amounts of data and relationships among data. For example this generalization contains the specific concepts of "art," "music," "architecture," "food," "clothing," "sports," and "customs." Implicit concepts in it are "society," "culture," "needs," "wants," "recreation," and "leisure." Other concepts can be generated.

The student in learning this generalization is considering various concrete and abstract concepts. He asks questions in order to comprehend the relationships that exist in the generalization. For the student to really comprehend the generalization, the teacher must provide numerous situations in which the student can analyze various data in order to discriminate commonalities and classify observed reality. The student requires opportunities to test the definitions that he has gained primarily through verbal means. The student must ask numerous questions concerning the concepts contained in the generalization in order to comprehend the generalization. The student also needs to pose questions as to the effectiveness of his means of investigation.

In dealing with generalizations, the student can consider entirely new complex situations and begin to organize the data into various classes. In working with generalizations, the student can obtain understanding with greater ease. He does not need to react to each individual fact; rather he can react to various classes of information and then analyze relationships.

Generalizations enable the student to learn about his world and enable us to teach. Much of what we present in the classroom is conceptual information. We talk of society having needs and of people living in houses. We assume student knowledge of the concepts "society," "needs," and "house." Often we use concepts without thought and mistake them for specific facts.

In dealing with concepts and generalizations, the student is active. This does not mean that he must discover everything through observation and questioning. The teacher can present many concepts verbally. However, the student should realize that he is dealing with classes of data termed "concepts" and that these classes can stress relationships in equations we call "generalizations." Simply put, a student can learn from both inductive and deductive teaching.

INDUCTIVE-DEDUCTIVE TEACHING— PLACE OF QUESTIONS

In inductive teaching the teacher guides pupils from dealing with specific facts to dealing with concepts and, finally, to concluding with generalizations. Questions are part of each stage of this process. Pupils consider specific factual material and organize obtained data into various classes or meaningful groupings. For example, a teacher wishing pupils to understand the geographic concept of "perpetual change" can structure situations in which pupils consider specific information relating to their environment. Pupils can study photographs of a particular town at different periods of time: turn of the century, thirty years later, ten years ago, the present. They can compare the pictures for similarities and differences. In this instance, the pupils discern that the particular town has changed drastically. But to recognize change is not sufficient; pupils need to question why various changes occurred. Could the changes have been stopped? In this questioning situation, pupils become analytical.

In inductive teaching, pupils investigate specific data, discover relationships and class data into conceptual groupings, and finally formulate generalizations. Pupils function somewhat as scholars, not to memorize but to comprehend knowledge more completely.

Pupils can still ask questions and not be experiencing inductive teaching. David Ausubel[7] argued that it was unproductive for an individual to rediscover everything. There is a place for providing information to the child verbally. Generalizations can be presented for consideration. The important point in presenting a generalization is to ascertain that pupils realize that the statement is a generalization. We must guide pupils to consider the underlying concepts and various supporting specific facts within it. If pupils merely memorize such statements to regurgitate them later on a test but do not learn their deeper meanings, they are inhibited from transferring any knowledge they might have gained to other situations. Pupils should acquire an understanding of the underlying concepts; they should realize the different relationships present among concepts and facts.

[7] David P. Ausubel, *The Psychology of Meaningful Verbal Learning* (New York: Grune & Stratton, 1963).

Inductive and deductive teaching are not alien if we consider inductive and deductive thinking as complementary parts of a continuous cognitive process. In deductive teaching, pupils confront a major premise or generalized body of information. The effective teacher leads pupils to analyze critically the major premise, a generalization, and apply it to numerous situations. For example, students presented the generalization that "man's consideration for the welfare of his fellowman is relatively recent from a time standpoint" are provided with situations where man's behavior is analyzed and finally judged in light of the generalization. The teacher guides and provides specific information where necessary. He asks questions and encourages pupils to ask questions.

In considering today's emphasis on the process of learning and the place of questions, we need to be more concerned with why we are using particular questions and particular strategies than with tallying the amount of time we are teaching in either a deductive or inductive mode. The particular teaching strategy employed should be determined by the particular objective or group of objectives being stressed. However, good questions must be part of whatever strategy we select.

QUESTIONS—THEIR POSITION IN THE EDUCATIONAL ENVIRONMENT

Questions should play a vital role in pupils' learning. However, research evidences that teachers and pupils have not been asking powerful questions. Teachers and pupils need to comprehend how to structure questions.

Within the context of a group learning situation, one prime means by which an individual can express autonomy—by which he can influence the nature of the instruction—is to ask questions.[8]

---

[8] Ben B. Strasser, *Components in a Teaching Strategy* (San Anselmo, Calif: Search Models Unlimited, 1967), p. 8.

They must be cognizant that questions help focus their think-ing. Questions demanding only specific facts will not enable teachers or pupils to synthesize numerous plans of action.

Teachers and pupils who comprehend the various types of questions can control their inquiry. Teachers will use ap-plication questions in activities that apply skills or information to new situations. Pupils can learn that certain types of ques-tions will enable them to achieve particular goals more effec-tively than other types of questions. For instance, pupils may wish to discover why people live in the mountains of South America. If they only ask questions at the specific fact level, they most likely will obtain specific information indicating that people do live in the mountains of South America. They will know that people live in these mountains because the text-book author or the teacher so informed them; they will lack real understanding of the reasons explaining this population distribution. However, if pupils formulate questions that ana-lyze elements and relationships among elements such as: What minerals do these people use? Why do the people use the minerals present as they do? How do the activities of the people indicate adjustment to the local environment? What are some causal relations between cultural mores and utilization of the environment?, they possess guides for gaining a rather complete understanding of this and similar situations.

Questions enable pupils to investigate productively. Ques-tions can guide pupils' thinking as they proceed from examin-ing specific facts to analyzing and evaluating generalized statements and vice versa. Questions, as Taba[9] has stated, can serve in lifting the level of thought in the learning process.

Implications for Teachers

Since effective questions and questioning strategies are integral parts of good teaching and learning, we as teachers need to plan our questions carefully. This does not mean script writing;

[9] Hilda Taba, *Teachers' Handbook for Elementary Social Studies*, intro. ed. (Reading, Mass.: Addison-Wesley Publishing Co., 1967), p. 122.

that would negate creative teaching. However, it does mean planning our questions: we must think through our interrogative dialogue.

Working with Questions in a Discovery Technique

When considering new strategies of teaching and techniques for learning, we focus on the process of learning. However, the process is not an end in itself. Process is utilized to provide a more comprehensive understanding of content whether at the concept or generalization level. Process also enables one to attend to the affective domain.

Process and Content

In much current discussion of process and content there appears some confusion. Parker and Rubin clarify this confusion by providing a precise distinction between the terms "process" and "content."

When the school specialist speaks of "content," he refers to the compendium of information which comprises the learning material for a particular course or a given grade. The information may consist of a related body of facts, laws, theories, and generalizations, as in a traditional science course, or a description of events, as in a history course, or in any other predetermined arrangement of a particular segment of man's knowledge.[10]

"Process" . . . refers to all the random, or ordered, operations which can be associated with knowledge and with human activities. There are a variety of processes through which knowledge is created. There are also processes for utilizing knowledge and for communicating it. Processes are involved in arriving at decisions, in evaluating consequences, and in accommodating new insights.[11]

"Content" refers to the accumulation of facts, concepts, and generalizations. "Process" refers to techniques of dealing

[10] J. Cecil Parker and Louis J. Rubin, *Process as Content: Curriculum Design and the Application of Knowledge* (Chicago: Rand McNally & Co., 1966), p. 1.

[11] Ibid., p. 2.

with content in ways producing new and clearer understandings. It should be stressed that content is used here to include facts, concepts, and generalizations. The question exists as an integral part of process.

But students require more than exposure to process to ask effective questions. Parker and Rubin[12] speak of the principle of cross-application. They stress that knowing processes does not guarantee their intelligent use. Intelligent use results from a curriculum that incorporates only those forms of knowledge possessing general applicability and which involves pupils in learning only those processes that possess the greatest amount of usefulness. To assure transfer of process knowledge, pupils need to be aware of the nature of a particular process or processes. How did the process evolve? Who in the past used this process and what were the results? What are some ways of using the process in the future? Pupils need to know ways of using process in different situations and how to adjust the method to situational demands. Pupils need to assess the process's effectiveness.[13] All these considerations center pupils' attention on questions.

Knowledge of process, with the underlying knowledge of questions, can exist at three levels: a knowing level, an understanding level, and a doing level. The first level is an awareness of the process; the second level is the ability to verbalize the process; the last level connotes being able to employ the process. Teachers need to plan both content and experiences to facilitate pupils' engagement at this third level.

PLANNING THE USE OF QUESTIONS

Intelligent selection of content and process and the designating of related questions results from careful diagnosis of the goals of the local and larger society, of the school, and of the needs of the students. The discovery curriculum requires that stu-

---

[12] Ibid., pp. 12-13.
[13] Ibid., p. 13.

dents be involved in their learning. However, not all students need to be active in the same ways. One needs to consider the ways by which individuals learn. How students approach problems, apply principles, synthesize data, and evaluate conclusions varies among individuals. Knowledge of such variation should enable us to individualize instruction.

Content Selection

Educators should ascertain those content samples that will motivate and meet individual needs. This content selection is crucial for it suggests appropriate processes and questions. Generalizations need first consideration; these abstractions represent relationships among concepts and so determine or suggest pertinent concepts for consideration.

Generalizations and their related concepts are the tentative end products; specific facts are selected as supportive of these abstractions. While affective learnings also are to be considered, this text stresses the cognitive domain.

Usually several content samples are considered for pupil consideration. Not all students need to study identical content in order to arrive at a concept or generalization. For example, one student could comprehend the concept of freedom through studying the American Revolution, while another could deduce the same concept through studying political struggles in Panama. The important goal is that students understand the concept and not just verbalize it. Moreover, the content samples selected must allow student engagement and be relevant to student needs. Students must have the opportunity to respond to the teacher's questions and to pose questions of their own.

Heuristic (Key) Questions

The term "heuristic" refers to the approach one takes in solving problems. Heuristic questions are capable of directing pupils' discovery or problem-solving approaches. Heuristic questions should be considered along with the content selected. Heuristic questions can be developed along with what Taba terms a "cognitive map."

In dealing with heuristic questions, we need to consider the avenues of thought such questions will trigger in children. We need to consider potential questions that will be raised by these initial questions. Usually key questions act as stimuli in initiating inquiry. But such inquiry will be short-lived if we have neglected considering other questions that pupils are likely to pose when engaged with the material.

Heuristic questions can provide focus; they can raise pupils' levels of thinking. Such questions even can suggest types of materials or activities to be employed. The use of heuristic questions as suggestive of a lesson's direction leads to consideration of cognitive maps in planning student learning.

Cognitive Maps

Taba[14] made a major contribution in developing the concept of cognitive maps. She considered two types of maps: a content map and a process map. The content map perfects the outline format. It indicates content samples supporting crucial ideas to be developed.

Organizing content and/or processes in a map format differentiates relevant from irrelevant information and organizes clearly information potentially useful to students in developing an information basis.

According to Taba,[15] cognitive maps can assume several forms. They can emphasize major points, sequential steps in a teaching strategy, and diagrams of potential outcomes. A cognitive map schematically indicates the teacher's intentions regarding content, process, or teaching strategy. Figure 1.1 developed by Taba explains how one might develop a lesson in reaction to the heuristic question, What would happen to the way of life in the desert if adequate water were obtained?

[14] Taba, op. cit., pp. 63-67.
[15] Ibid., p. 64.

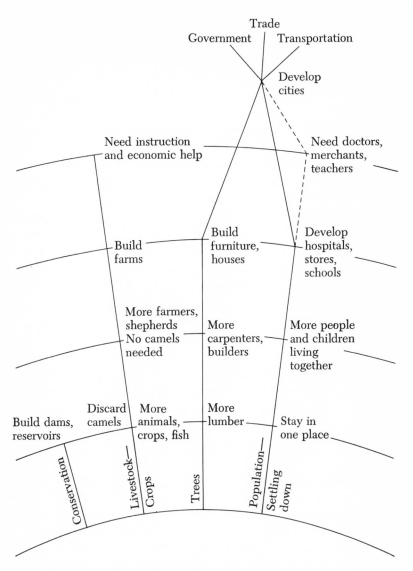

NOTE: The vertical lines describe the divergent lines of production; the horizontal lines describe the levels of "leaps" in these predictions.

SOURCE: Hilda Taba, *Teachers' Handbook for Elementary Social Studies* (Reading, Mass.: Addison-Wesley, 1967), p. 65.

Figure 1.1 Cognitive Map of Content in Third-Grade Discussion
Question: What would happen to the way of life in the desert
if sufficient water became available?

The vertical lines in the map represent avenues of divergent thought. These are possible ways in which students can pursue their inquiry. It should be pointed out that this is a major distinction between a map and an outline. Although it can provide for various samplings of contents, an outline usually cannot illustrate effectively various avenues of thought. A map can show several ways to plan situations having potential to lead pupils to discover numerous answers to questions. The answer one might accept as being most warranted depends greatly upon the data processed and the goals of the inquiry.

The horizontal lines represent levels of either cognitive thought or levels of abstraction. For example, in Figure 1.1 the first horizontal line at the left lists "Build dams, reservoirs." This could represent an end to that avenue of thought in relation to the topic of conservation. It does not exhibit a very high cognitive level even though the information is significant.

On the same horizontal line, the phrase "More lumber" written through the line indicates that the inquiry did not stop at that level. It continued to another level focusing on "More carpenters, builders" which then led to the third level representing an inference about the building needs for furniture and houses. This particular level then led into consideration of government, trade, and transportation.[16]

Why should teachers devote time to construct what one might call a "graphic outline"? The prime reason is that it suggests potential directions or avenues for pupils' investigations; further, it facilitates our anticipation of the possible avenues pupil discovery will assume. Also, it enables the teacher to contemplate possible questions and possible answers resulting from pupils' considering data.

Working with Cognitive Maps

Such maps can be used in numerous ways. They can indicate ways of organizing the sequential steps in a teaching strategy. This use really eliminates the schematic drawing. In this case, the map just lists the teacher's plans regarding major activities

[16] Ibid., pp. 63-66.

and key questions. After one activity group is completed, the teacher then plans the next in the sequence. Again, key, or heuristic, questions are listed. This particular map organization resembles quite closely an outline or even the standard lesson plan.

An example of organizing a map in this way follows. It deals with information relating to cattle ranching in Texas. This outline lists how pupils most likely will deal with the information and related questions.

COGNITIVE MAP REGARDING CATTLE RANCHING IN TEXAS

1. Organize the class into teams of two. Each team will select beef culture in Texas and investigate it in relation to the key questions. The questions at this level are used to frame the pupils' inquiry. The teaming is to help the pupils challenge each other's thinking.
   a. What is the climate like in the parts of Texas where beef cattle are raised?
   b. How large is the cattle industry in Texas?
   c. What type of capital does one need to engage in this type of agriculture?
   d. How did beef culture get started in Texas?
2. After these questions have been asked, the students should have a base for dealing with abstract information.
   Students now plan ways to accumulate information on beef culture and to test out tentative hunches concerning such economic activity. Students can investigate beef culture in other parts of the world to see if some of their ideas hold up with regard to Texas beef culture. Also the students can view films, study graphs, read agriculture reports, and study maps. Here they will be dealing with information at a higher level, or the second horizontal level, if working on a schematic representation.
   Continuing their work, the students may wish to consider the following questions:
   a. How does beef culture in Texas compare with that in other parts of the world?
   b. What data have you thus far obtained that provides the most insight into beef culture?
   c. How can your investigation be organized to use available materials and time efficiently?

     d. What are some common characteristics of beef culture that will help you formulate some concepts about this activity?

3. The students, using notes gathered from individual and team investigation, will formulate this information into statements that they will then present to the class as members of various committees. The presentations will be made to provide some tentative conclusions and to have such conclusions challenged. Also, suggestions can be made as to ways the information might be researched further. Emphasis upon synthesis and evaluation will be part of this level of activity. Questions receiving focus are as follows:

     a. Is beef culture the most effective use of the resources of this area of Texas?

     b. What ways can you suggest to improve the quality of beef culture in Texas?

     c. How can one best utilize the transportation and technology of the region in relation to beef culture?

     d. What can you say about how the people of this region interpret their resources? This question requires the pupils to derive an abstract relationship from among the data. Basically this is asking pupils to discover a generalization, which is the central reason for the entire lesson—to have the pupils discover the basic generalization that each culture tends to view its physical habitat in relation to its needs, resources, and level of technology.

Student Use

Students also can plan their own discovery sequences using cognitive maps. Students can formulate basic questions and possible avenues of investigation. They can enumerate potential activities. They also can plug into the map the various types of materials required and the types of situations needed for interaction with the materials. If we can use maps in planning teaching, students can use them for planning their own learning.

    Students also can use the cognitive map to check the effectiveness of their investigation in much the same way as the teacher constructs the map to diagnose the effectiveness of his lesson. Pupils pursuing independent inquiry need to develop skills of self-analysis. The cognitive map, especially the format that includes key questions, can serve to motivate learning. Each level of the map can focus the student's attention at increasingly complex and abstract levels of data. A definite focus is a prime requirement for effective inquiry; this use of the cognitive map seems to satisfy that prerequisite.

Reaction Avenues—Formulating Questions

In discovery curricula, questions are used to guide pupils in obtaining new insights, concepts, and generalizations. In using cognitive maps and in what I call reaction avenues, the teacher is planning for students' reactions. He is structuring questions to anticipate with some certainty the various avenues pupils will take in dealing with a particular subject.

Teaching is a decision-making process. To make an intelligent decision, one should trace to some extent the consequences of alternative lines of action. One must visualize possible outcomes that will result from pupil interaction with the curriculum. If the teacher has no idea of possible outcomes nor any idea of objectives and ways to achieve them, then what happens in the classroom is pure accident; he can take no credit for teaching. If learning has taken place, the pupil deserves sole praise.

Developing reaction avenues does not mean rigid planning. Rather, the teacher who has considered alternative outcomes becomes more receptive to student demands and needs. He has planned possible variations of the lesson to meet individual needs. Perhaps one student having difficulties in dealing with particular conceptual material requires a certain sequence of questions for effective learning. Time permitting, it is conceivable to sequence questions for each pupil so that he learns optimally.

Such suggestions might be criticized as script writing; this is not the intention. Script writing would stultify a lesson when flexibility is required. Student-teacher interaction would then be artificial. Writing and sequencing questions in reaction avenues is a suggestive device. The teacher never memorizes the questions. He will probably never use the exact questions in his teaching. Rather than providing him with a particular dialogue, the questions assist the teacher in considering the best possible ways to involve pupils. The teacher also employs such questions as stimuli to his own thinking.

EXAMPLE

Suppose a teacher plans for pupils to discover the generalization that man's use of natural resources is related to his desires and his level of technology. He decides to do this by studying industry in New England from 1880 to 1960. Assume the lesson is geared for either fourth or fifth grade. The teacher might first construct a data chart considering possible major areas for study. Two time periods, the 1880s and the 1960s, are chosen for study. To gain understanding of these two particular periods the students will have to consider times before and after these particular dates. The data chart might look like the one on the following page.[17]

Because the chart is sketchy, the teacher would need to add much detail. Under each section of the data chart, the teacher could list possible questions to guide students in considering how technology affects a particular region's economy. For instance, under "Industry," the teacher might list specific factual questions such as, How many textile factories did New England have in 1880? Where were most of these factories located? A higher level question could be, What would be some possible reasons for the location of the various textile factories? In what way did transportation routes affect the number of textile factories? How large were most of the textile factories? Out of what materials were the factories made? Did the factories have electricity? How did people get from one part of a textile factory to another?

Focusing on technology, the teacher could formulate questions relating to machines used in textile mills. What were the

---

[17] The idea of a retrieval chart was developed by Hilda Taba. The terms "data chart" and "data retrieval chart" are used interchangeably in this text.

INDUSTRY IN NEW ENGLAND 1880–1960

TIME	INDUSTRY	NEEDED TECHNOLOGY	LABOR AND FACILITIES REQUIRED	MARKET
1880	Textile	looms spinning jenny cotton gin water electricity (*power, resources, capital*)	cheap labor skilled labor factory space (*specialization of labor*)	wool market cotton market large numbers of people (*market*) (*desires*) (*needs*) (*goods*) (*services*) (*exchange*)
1960	Electronics	vacuum tube transistors circuits sterile compartments	available factory space from shut-down textile mills— no need to build new factories	urban area national and worldwide market (*desires*) (*needs*)
			university consultants available (*specialization of labor*)	space program, radio, TV large numbers of people using these materials (*goods*) (*services*)
				air transportation (*present growth of market exchange*)

NOTE: Concepts relating to economics are in parentheses.

names of these machines? What powered most of these machines? How many people worked these machines? What were the specific functions of these machines? Where were these machines made? Of what materials were the machines made? How were the machines arranged in the factory? Were machines arranged by function in the factory? What would happen if the machines were arranged differently?

These questions could be ordered in a particular sequence. The teacher would probably have to experiment to find the most productive sequence. Initially one might ask questions dealing with specific facts, then one might phrase questions utilizing these facts. If students already possess a strong data base, initial questions can focus on utilizing information. For example, in discussing technology needed for an 1880 textile factory, one might direct questions at identifying the names of the different machines, the locations of the factories, and the numbers of people involved in working the machines before initiating questions requiring pupils to analyze the relationship of factory location to types of machines used, to consider technological specialization, and to evaluate if the factories effectively used machines. Here attention could be directed to how the level of technology affected how one used the natural power resources of New England. The concepts of power and capital could be considered.

Considering labor, the teacher could construct sample questions. How many people were needed to run a textile factory? What types of skills did these people need? Who trained these people? What salaries did these people earn? Where did the laborers come from? Again, higher level questions would be formulated after asking these knowledge questions. Attention could center on the concept of specialization and how specialization of labor affects production.

Next, market is considered, starting with rather specific questions aimed at guiding pupils in investigating the facts regarding market and the demand for textiles. Here the basic concept of conflict between unlimited wants and limited resources could be introduced. What types of cloth were produced in these mills? How many people were in the immediate areas to buy these textiles? Did the people in the adjoining urban areas have sufficient money to purchase these textiles? What did cotton and woolen cloth cost in 1880? What types of clothing did people wear in 1880? What were the styles? Some of these questions could also deal with the concept of market and related concepts of goods and services. The concepts of supply and demand, labor, capital, and urban area also could be considered. Such concept blending enables the teacher to get at the structure of economics.

After studying New England industry in 1880, pupils could investigate the electronics industry of New England in the 1960s. Again, the teacher could use the same sections of the data chart. Under "Industry," the teacher might frame questions such as, What were the major electronics industries in New England in 1960? What were their names? What types of products were produced? Where were the major firms located?

Under "Needed Technology," questions could direct pupils to consider inventions required before the industry could be established. What are some of the specific machines needed in the production of a vacuum tube? What power demands are exerted by modern industry? What capital outlays are needed for modern technology?

Under the "Labor" category, questions could deal with skilled labor (focusing on specialization), available factory space, and the numerous universities in the Northeast area. Sample questions could be, What relationships exist between the electronics firms and the number of universities? How are university scientists involved in the electronics industry? What types of skills are required of the factory workers? Again the questions start at a rather specific level. However, later questions could relate to the concept "specialization" and the fact that specialization necessitates market. Under "Market," questions could stimulate pupils to analyze relationships or synthesize their data. What is the current status of the electronics industry? What are some relationships between government funding of space activities and this industry? How does this industry relate to the total economy? The later questions attempt to have pupils focus on key concepts and relationships. Such attention to concepts and relationships is what is meant by structure.

Comparison

After these two depth studies, the teacher can list questions to compare New England industry in 1880 with New England industry in 1960. These questions would be phrased to encourage pupils to analyze differences, to make comparisons, and to interpret the findings in light of the major objective of the study, that of generalizing that man utilizes his natural resources in relation to his desires and level of technology.

Questions at this point of the lesson could be: How did the factories of 1880 compare with those of 1960? What machines did each type of factory need? What similar needs existed with regard to labor? What differences existed? What can you say about the relationships of factory location to topographic features? Did the relationships change over the period of time considered? How did the market for textiles in 1880 differ from the market for electronics in 1960? How were the markets alike? What are some general statements we can make about market and about man's needs and desires? What can we say about the use of transportation systems during these two periods? Would you say that industry in New England in 1880 and in 1960 was effectively using its resources? In general, what can we say about how man uses his resources in relation to his technology?

In this phase, questions are aimed primarily at having pupils use information gathered at the other two phases of depth study. Questions are not aimed at just gathering knowledge; this has been done. This phase directs students in synthesizing information. The teacher is a guide, a motivator, a co-ordinator, a manager.

Constructing Reaction Avenues

For each subsection of a data retrieval chart, the teacher or student can construct a tentative reaction avenue. What potential directions for thought can questions suggest?

The teacher can construct the following reaction avenue, which deals with the technology needed for an 1880 textile factory.

The solid lines indicate the most likely direction of the discovery session; the broken lines suggest divergent investigation.

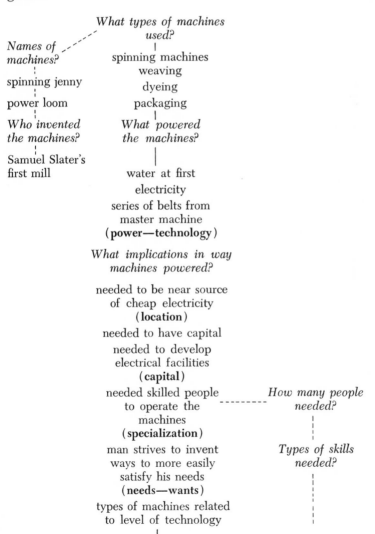

What types of machines used?

Names of machines?

spinning machines

spinning jenny

weaving

power loom

dyeing

packaging

Who invented the machines?

What powered the machines?

Samuel Slater's first mill

water at first

electricity

series of belts from master machine
(**power—technology**)

What implications in way machines powered?

needed to be near source of cheap electricity
(**location**)

needed to have capital

needed to develop electrical facilities
(**capital**)

needed skilled people to operate the machines
(**specialization**)

How many people needed?

man strives to invent ways to more easily satisfy his needs
(**needs—wants**)

Types of skills needed?

types of machines related to level of technology

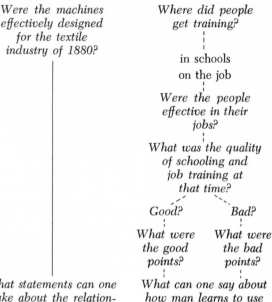

Were the machines
effectively designed
for the textile
industry of 1880?

Where did people
get training?

in schools
on the job

Were the people
effective in their
jobs?

What was the quality
of schooling and
job training at
that time?

Good?   Bad?

What were   What were
the good   the bad
points?   points?

What statements can one
make about the relation-
ship between man and
machines, between
technology and man,
between technology and
man's desires?

What can one say about
how man learns to use
technology?

Key:
- - - - - - - - (possible branch investigations)
—————— (main stream of reaction)

As stated previously, from designing reaction avenues we can anticipate directions of investigation. By such planning we can schedule appropriate learning activities, places to conduct the activities, and necessary support materials. We can anticipate where certain students can function most effectively in the investigation. For instance, if one student owns a model of an electric generator, he can serve as a data source on machine power. If another student has a small hand loom, he can act as a resource person on looms. Studying avenues of potential reaction can suggest numerous effective ways to deal with topics.

Isn't this too difficult for children?

One might consider reaction avenues desirable for intermediate and upper-grade students but too complex for primary-level children. However, children in the primary grades are thinking and certainly ask questions.

Consider a teacher planning a unit about families around the world. The teacher devises a depth study of two family groups, the child's own and an Indian family of the Amazon basin. One subtopic of the unit deals with why people wear clothes and the types of clothing worn. The teacher constructs a data retrieval chart in outline form. An outline makes it easier for the child to compare his family with the Amazon family.

CLOTHES

My Family	*Amazon Family*
I. What clothes are worn?	I. What clothes are worn?
A. for school	A. for school
girls—dresses boys—long pants jackets hats kerchiefs	(no school) girls and boys few if any clothes beads, paint
B. for play	B. for play
in summer—shorts and shirts, blouses, dresses, slacks in winter—snowsuits, boots, raincoats. etc.	no clothes most of the time paint boys might wear shorts at certain times leaves
C. for sleep	C. for sleep
pajamas, nightgowns blankets	perhaps leaves mosquito nets nothing light blankets
D. for church	D. religious services
suits flowered hats for girls	paint, special masks, feathers beads

While this outline is not complete, it does list some specific facts for which questions could be written. These questions would guide pupils in their search for data and could stimulate related investigations. The teacher can list certain questions dealing with why boys and girls in the United States wear what they do when playing. Why do both boys and girls wear sneakers when they play in summer? Why do boys and girls in the Amazon wear beads and little or no clothing when playing? The emphasis here is on the "why" behind such dress. What can one say about the function of clothing? Which group of parents is dressing their children more sensibly? These questions are aimed at comparing, synthesizing, and evaluating information. Of course, at the primary level the comparisons and evaluations are not sophisticated; nevertheless, children are still working with data. The teacher is not supplying all answers. The children can experience the excitement of discovering relationships among information.

Under each of these headings the teacher can devise a possible reaction avenue. From considering peoples' dress for church or religious services, the teacher can deal with how culture is expressed through dress for special occasions. We dress up to go to church and the Amazon people dress or "paint up" to recognize their spirits or gods. This illustrates that in church or a religious occasion one shows the seriousness of the occasion by his personal appearance.

The chart can suggest activities as well as questions. For example, one can present pictures of people dressed in certain ways and have the children guess what they are doing or what jobs they have. Or pupils can observe articles of clothing or certain body decorations and decide who would wear these clothes or decorations: a man? woman? boy? girl? The lesson would aim at getting pupils to realize a generalization or generalizations about clothing, why people wear clothing, and how culture and local environment affect clothing types.

It should be restressed that in making various data charts and formulating questions to accompany them, one does not expect children to use the discovery approach full time. One can devise such charts and still provide information in a deductive manner.

Effective Questioner

Effective materials and potentially stimulating situations will be of no value if the teacher lacks skills in formulating questions and using various questioning strategies. Questions must serve as guides by which students develop more in-depth perceptions. The teacher can and must ask questions that enable students to use him as a sounding board. The teacher can phrase questions to act as a catalyst to students' thinking. The teacher can formulate questions that direct and guide students in various avenues of search. Of course, the teacher can use questions as lesson motivators; questions can supply the focus for an investigation.

If the teacher uses questions in such ways, students will discover that the question is a most valuable learning tool. It is a device to organize their thinking to achieve their objectives. Students asking questions as they deal with various learning situations provide themselves with data or an awareness of deficits in data. Such knowledge is essential if students are to assume major roles in their learning.

Teachers can use questions not only to see if students have certain data at hand but to get students to be cognizant of why they are dealing with data in certain ways. The intent of a student's investigation can be considered. Often, confronting a student with questions as to why he wants certain information enables him to discover the irrelevancy of his pursuit. The teacher provides students with an understanding of the nature of the question and how to utilize particular questions to obtain certain types of data.

STUDENT FUNCTIONING IN A DISCOVERY CURRICULUM

Students should assume much of the initiative for their own learning. They should be active rather than passive in their educational experience. In this way they not only achieve insights as to processes to use and questions to ask, but they learn to apply them in similar situations. The core of all process learning relates to the principles and techniques used in research. These techniques of problem identification, experimentation, measurement, and conclusion comprise what is known as scientific method. There is no one scientific method, but there exist similarities in the techniques employed by scientists.

The steps of problem solving or any version of scientific method are not programmed in a tight sequence that an individual follows with little thought. Students or scientists engaged in investigation often jump from stage to stage as they deal with data. At each stage careful attention is given to data and to the particular process being employed in investigation. Often one has to go back to prior stages.

The terms "discovery," "inquiry," "scientific method," and "problem solving" are often used with little precision. There is in my opinion no great difference between "discovery" and "inquiry." Inquiry is a composite of many behaviors used when investigating something. Suchman[18] has a type of inquiry. Goldmark[19] lists steps of inquiry. Michaelis[20] discusses three types of inquiry. Rather than search for a precise type, one needs to analyze the several types to identify common elements. Then the general stages discussed below are sufficient to give us an idea of what students should do, albeit in a flexible manner, when working with questions in a discovery curriculum.

Stages of Activity

Students should utilize knowledge to achieve greater insights. In gaining a knowledge base, they can be active or passive.

[18] J. Richard Suchman, *Developing Inquiry* (Chicago: Science Research Associates, 1966).

[19] Bernice Goldmark, *Social Studies–A Method of Inquiry* (Belmont, Calif.: Wadsworth Publishing Co., 1968), pp. 116-18.

[20] John U. Michaelis, chairman, *Social Sciences Education Framework for California Public Schools* (Sacramento, Calif.: Report of the Statewide Social Sciences Study Committee, California State Board of Education, 1968).

They can search out specific facts and information or the teacher can present it to them.

After gaining sufficient specific data, students begin to further clarify or identify their focus. Throughout the process they are thinking, raising questions. They may identify or formulate a problem or a discrepancy between information previously held and presently gained. This first stage, if the students are active in gathering the data, requires skill in analyzing content and situations. It necessitates students asking appropriate questions.

Once students have acquired a sufficient factual base and identified a problem focus, they can usually formulate, with teacher guidance, ways of further investigation. This is creative thinking, which can appear at several levels of discovery.

The next stage is conducting the investigation—testing hypotheses. During the investigation, the student functions at various cognitive levels. The student gathers data employing primary and secondary sources. He might interview certain people to gain their perceptions. He might read and extrapolate information from several charts, graphs, and tables. He might compare two or more maps to ascertain certain information.

Concluding this stage, the student must check his results. Here he engages critical thinking to validate his results. He analyzes the results for underlying assumptions. He separates the irrelevant data from the relevant. At this stage the student must do more than ascertain the accuracy of his findings. He must go beyond mere description of what charts report or what primary and secondary sources list. He must interpret. This is where concept and generalization formation appear. This is, according to Bloom, the level of synthesis. The student sorts data according to its commonality. Significant aspects of information are identified and various facts grouped under larger and more general groupings.

Synthesizing is essential in discovery learning. However, a student has not completed his active learning upon reaching a generalization. Is it valid? What is the power of the generalization? Is another investigation warranted to check out the results of this study? Here the student is evaluating the results of his inquiry.

SUMMARY

Questions hold the focal point in the discovery curriculum, in which students are challenged to participate actively in the learning process. The discovery curriculum also demands active teachers. We manage educational environments. We organize educational content and experiences for the pupils.

The question is a vital tool in the process of learning. But the question is not simply a few words with a question mark; it is complex and has diverse dimensions. The next chapter provides examples of questions which can help the student function primarily in the cognitive domain of learning. However, these question types also can stimulate student functioning in the affective domain.

2

Question Types

Knowing that questions are important is not enough. One needs to know how to plan effective questions. To do so one must understand the various types. Following are examples of questions according to one scheme.

A CLASSIFICATION SCHEME

Questions can be classified in several ways. I will use the categories of educational objectives as developed by Bloom—knowledge, comprehension, application, analysis, synthesis, and evaluation—for our study of questions.

An abbreviated version of this taxonomy follows.

TAXONOMY OF EDUCATIONAL OBJECTIVES
COGNITIVE DOMAIN

KNOWLEDGE

Knowledge

> Knowledge involves the recall of specifics and universals, the recall of methods and processes, or the recall of a pattern, structure, or setting.

Knowledge of Specifics

> The recall of specific and isolable bits of information.

Knowledge of Ways and Means
of Dealing with Specifics

> Knowledge of the ways of organizing, studying, judging, and criticizing.

Knowledge of the Universals
and Abstractions in a Field

> Knowledge of the major schemes and patterns by which phenomena and ideas are organized.

INTELLECTUAL ABILITIES AND SKILLS

Comprehension

This refers to a type of understanding or apprehension such that the individual knows what is being communicated and can make use of the material or idea being communicated without necessarily relating it to other material or seeing its fullest implications.

> *Translation*
>
> > Comprehension as evidenced by the care and accuracy with which the communication is paraphrased or rendered from one language or communication to another.
>
> *Interpretation*
>
> > The explanation or summarization of a communication.
>
> *Extrapolation*
>
> > The extension of trends or tendencies beyond the given data to determine implications, consequences, corollaries, effects, etc., which are in accordance with the conditions described in the original communication.

Application

The use of abstractions in particular and concrete situations. The abstractions may be in the form of general ideas, rules of procedures, or generalized methods.

Analysis

> The breakdown of a communication into its constituent elements or parts.

> > *Analysis of Elements*

> > > Identification of the elements included in a communication.

> > *Analysis of Relationships*

> > > The connections and interactions between elements and parts of a communication.

> > *Analysis of Organizational Principles*

> > > The organization, systematic arrangement, and structure which hold the communication together.

Synthesis

> The putting together of elements and parts so as to form a whole.

> > *Production of a Unique Communication*

> > > The development of a communication in which the writer or speaker attempts to convey ideas, feelings, and/or experiences to others.

> > *Production of a Plan, or
> > Proposed Set of Operations*

> > > The development of a plan or the proposal of a plan of operations.

> > *Derivation of a Set of Abstract Relations*

> > > The development of a set of abstract relations either to classify or explain particular data or phenomena, or the deduction of propositions and relations from a set of basic propositions or symbolic representations.

Evaluation

> Judgments about the value of material and methods for given purposes.

Judgments in Terms of Internal Evidence

Evaluation of the accuracy of a communication from such evidence as logical accuracy, consistency, and other internal criteria.

Judgments in Terms of External Criteria

Evaluation of material with reference to selected or remembered criteria.

SOURCE: Condensed from Benjamin S. Bloom et al., eds., *Taxonomy of Educational Objectives: Handbook I, The Cognitive Domain* (New York: David McKay Co., 1956), pp. 201-7. Used by permission of David McKay Company, Inc.

Inherent in a taxonomy is that the higher levels subsume the lower ones. Thus comprehension subsumes knowledge; application subsumes comprehension and knowledge; analysis subsumes application, comprehension, and knowledge; synthesis subsumes analysis, application, comprehension, and knowledge. Finally, evaluation subsumes all the lower levels. This hierarchical nature of the taxonomy is important to remember when formulating questions at the various levels or when determining objectives at a particular level. Objectives and supporting questions at the analysis level not only will guide students in analysis but also will challenge them to function at the levels of application, comprehension, and knowledge. Indeed, one cannot analyze information without using some skills, without comprehending some materials or situations, and certainly not without having some base data. This last point should reassure those who are particularly concerned with their pupils acquiring sufficient basic factual information. Good questions will assist this factual base gathering and make the experience more meaningful.

Because of the emphasis on discovery methods and teaching students how to deal effectively with data, we need to use the right types of questions. If we understand Bloom's taxonomy, we can use it as a guide to formulating more appropriate questions.

Types of Questions

Knowledge

Knowledge is the first level of the taxonomy[1] and provides the base for greater understanding.

Knowledge of Specifics

The most obvious aspect of knowledge is that of specific facts and terms. Knowledge at this level can be considered to comprise building blocks for later intellectual functioning. Questions at this level emphasize regurgitation of facts. This does not mean that these are poor questions and that such a stress is bad. The effectiveness of questions must be judged in relation to the objectives for a particular lesson. If our objective is to provide students with a data base, then knowledge questions that ask for specific facts are effective questions.

Questions of this kind are easy to formulate, and we rarely need practice in asking them. However, we should query our rationale for asking such questions. Just how is the response going to assist students in obtaining greater understanding of particular information?

EXAMPLES

1. What state grows the most lettuce?
2. Who were the first astronauts to step on the moon?
3. What do we call this type of instrument?
4. What is the earth's distance from the sun?

Knowledge of Ways and Means of Dealing with Specifics[2]

But the knowledge dimension is not solely concerned with specific facts. The second major division of knowledge centers on ways and means of dealing with specifics. Bloom[3] sub-

---

[1] Bloom, *Taxonomy*, p. 63.

[2] Ibid., p. 68.

[3] Ibid., pp. 69-74.

divides this second major category into knowledge of conventions, of trends and sequences, of classifications and categories, of criteria, and of methodology. The stress here is not solely on facts but rather on the knowledge of processes of dealing with facts.

In the first subdivision,[4] *knowledge of conventions*, the student is expected to be cognizant of accepted ways of dealing with various types of information or situations. Questions relating to how one constructs a sentence would be within this category. Questions in mathematics asking students the meaning of various symbols could also comprise this section.

EXAMPLES

1. What is the correct form for a business letter?
2. When a lady enters the room what should a gentleman do?
3. In making a speech what are three things we should remember?
4. Which is the correct spelling, "receive or "recieve"?

The second subdivision[5] relates to *knowledge of trends and sequences*. Questions at this level query students' knowledge of various phenomena in relation to a time dimension. The stress of these questions is not on whether students understand the trend but only that they recognize its existence.

EXAMPLES

1. What steps does one follow in directing a bill through Congress?
2. What can you say about population growth in the United States?
3. What were the events that led up to the Second World War?
4. How did the Crusades affect the development of western European commerce?

[4] Ibid., p. 69.
[5] Ibid., p. 70.

5. What statements can you make about peoples' rights in the United States during the last ten years?

The third subdivision[6] deals with *knowledge of classifications and categories*. Here stress is upon students remembering certain groupings of information. At this level students are not required to do anything with the categories; they are only asked to recall from memory certain classifications. They might be expected to give the various species of trees in the Northwest. Or perhaps the question requires a recall of the types of birds found in the Everglades.

EXAMPLES

1. What are the three main types of economic activity?
2. What are two categories of numbers?
3. Name some kinds of poems in English literature.
4. How many types of rocks do geologists recognize?
5. The discipline primarily concerned with man's relationship to his physical environment is
   a. history
   b. geography
   c. sociology
   d. economics
   e. anthropology

The fourth subdivision[7] deals with *knowledge of criteria*. Stress is on awareness of criteria developed. Perhaps the teacher has presented a list of criteria for judging the effectiveness of a painting. The teacher could ask for the regurgitation of such a list. With the stress on valuing in the schools the students need some knowledge of criteria.

EXAMPLES

1. What are three essential criteria for judging the effectiveness of a surrealist painting?
2. What criteria does the government use to determine if a family can be classified as living in poverty?

[6] Ibid., p. 71.
[7] Ibid., p. 72.

   3. Thomas Jefferson's consideration of the well-educated person involves what criteria?

The last subdivision[8] under ways and means of dealing with specifics concerns *knowledge of methodology*. This dimension is solely concerned with the student's awareness of several methods or processes, not in his ability to apply them to actual situations. The teacher may wish to ascertain a student's knowledge of the steps in problem-solving. Or perhaps he questions the student to determine if he knows the process he would use to solve a particular ecological problem. In responding to such questions the student might recall the different processes that scholars employ.

EXAMPLES

   1. What two process can a geographer employ in studying man and his environment?

   2. If a scientist wishes to grow bacteria, his first step is to
     a. isolate the bacteria
     b. prepare the petri dish for the introduction of the bacteria
     c. discuss the problem with his colleague
     d. prepare his time schedule for the experiment

   3. If a teacher wishes to individualize his instruction, his first step should be to
     a. select his materials
     b. consider his own competencies
     c. diagnose the abilities, needs, and interests of the pupils in his class
     d. get permission from the principal

   4. Which of the following is considered the most accurate way by which an archaeologist can determine the age of an artifact?
     a. determine the depth at which it was unearthed
     b. use the carbon test
     c. interview the person who unearthed it
     d. do a pollen analysis of the material

[8] Ibid., p. 73.

Knowledge of the Universals and Abstractions in a Field

Bloom's third major category of knowledge deals with knowledge of principles and generalizations and knowledge of theories and structures.[9] The sole requirement is that the student be cognizant of various abstractions, whether stating a generalization or recalling a theory. Questions at this level are asking only for awareness of diverse abstractions. Later questions might ask the student to apply or even to formulate such abstractions. When asking questions relating to theories or generalizations, we must not become misled into thinking that, since a student can respond to this level of question, he is dealing with data in an inductive manner. Being able to respond is only possessing knowledge; it is not using knowledge. Often pupils can verbalize generalizations without really comprehending them.

EXAMPLES

1. Which of the following is the best description of how man uses his natural resources?
   a. Man uses his resources in various ways according to his cultural interpretation of these resources.
   b. Man cannot use certain resources until society expresses a demand for them.
   c. The use of resources is usually closely tied to the economics of the particular time-period.
   d. The need for certain resources depends upon the creation of a felt need.
2. Which of the following statements of the relationship between market price and normal price is true?
   a. Over a short period of time, market price varies directly with changes in normal price.
   b. Over a long period of time, market price tends to equal normal price.
   c. Market price is usually lower than normal price.
   d. Over a long period of time, market price determines normal price.[10]

[9] Ibid., pp. 75-77.
[10] Ibid., p. 87. Reprinted by permission.

3. From the study of various cultures what can we say about the family?
   a. The family is the basic social unit in most cultures.
   b. The family is usually altered in various cultures.
   c. The family is usually both matriarchical and patriarchical in structure.
   d. Most children in the family have definite work roles.

4. What is the basic structure of the discipline of economics as presented in class?

Comprehension

Bloom's second level of educational objectives is *comprehension*. He states, "Here we are using the term 'comprehension' to include those objectives, behaviors, or responses which represent an understanding of the literal message contained in a communication."[11] Bloom has divided comprehension into three divisions: translation, interpretation, and extrapolation.

Translation

The first division, *translation*,[12] focuses on the student's ability to translate or paraphrase a communication from one form to another. It could consist of his translating an algebraic formula into a written statement. It could mean repeating what the author means in his own words. At this level knowledge is required, but the stress is on employing this knowledge to understand a particular material.

EXAMPLES

1. A teacher is diagnosing the abilities of his students and appraising his materials and the school facilities. In which activity is this person most likely engaging?
   a. evaluating progress
   b. planning a lesson
   c. self-diagnosis
   d. preparing for a parent-teacher conference

---

[11] Ibid., p. 89.
[12] Ibid., p. 91.

2. The idea systems of primitive groups of people are highly restricted and traditional in content and, in addition, have been transmuted into customary ways of doing things. This best illustrates—
   a. the stability of the primitive social organizations;
   b. how primitive people evaluate the worth of ideas;
   c. the change of ideas to action;
   d. the repetition of customary ways of doing things;
   e. the slow progress of primitive people.[13]

3. Translate this paragraph into French.

4. Looking at the demographic map on page 22, list the populations of the ten largest cities shown.

5. The curriculum should contain subject matter emphasizing the social experience of man, and the teacher should serve the role of a research project director. Which of the following philosophies does this statement represent?
   a. idealism
   b. realism
   c. experimentalism
   d. existentialism

6. Geographers are discussing the "press of people." What does this phrase mean?

7. In Edgar Allan Poe's poem "The Raven," he uses the phrase, "Quoth the Raven, 'Nevermore.'" Explain the symbolism of the raven and this phrase.

Interpretation

Bloom's second division of the level of comprehension is *interpretation*.[14] At this level the reader is to derive the essential meanings of a communication. He is asked to relate the different elements of the communication. Relationships which the author has developed should be clear to the reader. Interpretation is not solely related to understanding the written or spoken word. It can direct the student to understand the general meaning of various art works, or music, or events. Interpretation is an extension of the first comprehension level. The central question is not what did the author or material say, as in translation,

---

[13] Ibid., p. 99. Reprinted by permission.
[14] Ibid., p. 93.

but what is the basic idea or ideas, or message of the situation or writing.

Norris Sanders, who utilized the Taxonomy to expand on the topic of questions, states that the interpretative level of comprehension deals with six forms of relationships that can be found in materials:

1. comparative relationships (determining if ideas are identical, similar, different, unrelated, or contradictory)
2. relationships of implications
3. relationship of an inductive generalization to supporting evidence
4. relationship of a value, skill, or definition to an example of its use
5. numerical relationship
6. cause and effect relationship[15]

Sanders mentions that a significant characteristic of this level of comprehension is that the student either discovers or uses relationships on a common-sense level. His common-sense level is stressed as opposed to an analytical approach to these relationships, which would represent a higher level in Bloom's taxonomy, that of analysis.

EXAMPLES

1. Compare the use of natural resources in the United States with that in Brazil.
2. Consider the current social crisis in the urban areas. Drawing upon your text, what are some conclusions you can make?
3. Study the chart showing the increase in the number of cars being used in Washington state. From this chart, which of the following is the best judgment that one could make?
   a. The number of cars in the state will level out after more people arrive in the state;

[15] Sanders, *Classroom Questions. What Kinds?* (New York: Harper & Row, 1966), p. 43. Used by permission of Harper & Row, Publishers.

    b. The number of cars cannot be allowed to increase without control;

    c. The number of cars in the state will require higher gasoline taxes;

    d. The number of cars in the state will mean additional revenue for the state.

4. Study the chart showing the number of man-hours required to buy three electric appliances—TV, washing machine, stereo—in 1950 and 1970. What are some basic statements that can be made from studying this chart?

5. The radical left and radical right are at opposite poles at first consideration. In what ways are these two groups similar to each other? Consult what you have read in your text in preparing your answer.

Sanders also identifies interpretation questions according to the format of the question: analogy, irrelevant item, and the scrambled outline.[16] With the analogy question, the student might recognize or comprehend the basic relationship between many types of data.

EXAMPLES

1. Lion is to pride as ———— is to flock.
2. Three is to nine as ———— is to twenty-four.

The irrelevant-item question requires the student to understand or interpret the relationship among various data in order to detect that which does not belong.

EXAMPLES

1. Which term does not belong in this sequence?
    a. region
    b. freedom
    c. power
    d. gold

2. Which of the following does not belong?
    a. geography
    b. biology

[16] Ibid., pp. 63–69.

c. reading
d. physics

The scrambled-outline question requires the student to comprehend the correct sequence or development of certain information or to understand the basic structure of certain material. Questions of this type can list in an incorrect sequence several events that have happened and ask children to re-arrange them correctly.

EXAMPLES

1. The book lists the major events concerned with the American Revolution. These are listed in incorrect order. Rearrange the list in chronological order and determine which are major events and which are minor or supporting events.
   Tax on tea
   Sons of Liberty rebel
   Revolution
   Navigation Acts
   Closing port of Boston
   Continental Congress
   Franklin urges people to unite
   King George shows that he has power to tax

Extrapolation

Extrapolation is Bloom's third level of comprehension.[17] Questions at this level not only ask students to translate and gain a basic understanding of the material or situation but require them to go beyond the situation. The student is asked to expand the information. If he has interpreted the basic relationships of a communication, then what might be the consequences of this relationship? Extrapolation is asking for an inference. However, the student should be cognizant of the limitations of his inference-making. This level of comprehension allows the student to interpolate data to make a meaningful continuum. The teacher asks such questions so that students will ask themselves, If this is what is present now, what may

[17] Bloom, *Taxonomy*, p. 95.

be said about the information at some future time? Drawing conclusions from reading various materials is the major emphasis of this level of comprehension.

EXAMPLES

1. From what the three speakers have said regarding the world's population, which of the following is the most likely conclusion?
   a. There is no need to fear the population explosion;
   b. Man's technology will keep up with the added pressures of more people;
   c. Man needs to be more effective in limiting his numbers;
   d. We have poor location of population rather than overpopulation.

2. From the three maps showing the migration of people in the United States, where do you think the greatest number of people will be living in the year 2000?
   a. West
   b. Midwest
   c. Northeast
   d. South

3. Look at the level of medicine today and the length of life among Americans. What effect will this relationship have on man's life span in thirty years?

Application

Application is the third level of educational objectives in Bloom's hierarchy.[18] We in education should desire students to do more than indicate their comprehension of information read or encountered in the classroom. Our objective should focus on having the student apply what he has learned to other situations and learning tasks. Application is a crucial aspect of the discovery curriculum, for it requires a student to use his information. Exactly how the student should function with his information is not explicitly told him. Part of the challenge lies in the student's being able to determine the appropriate

[18] Ibid., p. 120.

process to use. The student himself must judge what study skills or types of thinking he needs in order to respond to a question. The central thrust of the application question is that the pupil deals with data or solves some type of problem.

Application questions can focus on a wide variety of student activities. The questions can ask students to apply a particular generalization to a particular situation confronting the local community, or to apply a particular skill acquired in mathematics to a new problem situation, or to apply their understanding of the democratic process to the organization of a class government, or to apply some scientific principle to a particular problem situation.

Application questions can provide students with opportunities to apply knowledge gained at the comprehension and knowledge levels. Often we educators, in our haste to cover the required material, only allow students to voice their comprehension. Application, since it requires additional time, is marked off as inappropriate activity. If we are to really have a discovery-oriented curriculum, we must schedule time for application of knowledge and skills acquired. In life, students will be tested as to how well they can apply their knowledge. We should not wait for students to graduate from formal school before allowing them opportunities to apply what they know to further increase their understanding.

EXAMPLES

1. An electric iron (110 volts, 1000 watts) has been used for some time and the plug contacts have become burned, thus introducing additional resistance. How will this affect the amount of heat which the iron produces?[19]

2. X and Y can do a piece of work together in 15 days. They work together for 6 days; then X quits and Y finishes the work in 30 more days. In how many days can Y do the piece of work alone? Show your work below.

[19] Ibid., p. 132. Reprinted by permission.

    a. 30
    b. 40
    c. 50
    d. 60
    e. none of the foregoing[20]

3. Looking at the map, state the possible locations for the cultivation of wheat.
4. Mr. Jones is going to locate a new steel plant in the state. Suggest three possible locations where he will be able to produce steel economically.
5. Look at the following paragraph and correctly identify those words that are serving the function of nouns.

Analysis

Analysis is the fourth level of Bloom's Taxonomy.[21] Bloom has divided this level into three parts: analysis of elements, analysis of relationships, and analysis of organizational principles. At this level the student is confronted with the task of diagnosing material or situations or environments and separating them into their component parts and focusing on the relationships between these parts to each other and with regard to the total structure organization. Bloom relates this level solely to materials that communicate. Sanders[22] in his treatment of this level also relates it to materials that communicate. I believe that the level also can and must be applied to the analysis of situations and various environments. For instance, students dealing with geographic phenomena in the open field can certainly ask themselves analysis questions directed to the identification of significant elements or phenomena in the particular environment or to the relationships that exist between such identified elements.

    Students studying the ills of society certainly can deal with analysis questions that focus on significant elements of

---

[20] Ibid., p. 133. Reprinted by permission.
[21] Ibid., p. 145.
[22] Sanders, *Classroom Questions*, p. 97.

society. It is much too narrow to assume that these questions only deal with the written word. We in education sometimes overstress the written word as the means by which man gains knowledge. Man can learn through observation of his environment and through observation of man's social groupings as well as from how others have recorded their perceptions.

Sanders states: "Analysis is different in that the thinking is relatively unfamiliar to many teachers and cannot be used until it is mastered on a deeper level than is possible to describe in this chapter."[23] Sanders mentions that the student at this level of the taxonomy must still be concerned with subject matter but, in addition, he must be conscious of the intellectual processes he is performing. He also must be cognizant of the rules for reaching a valid and true conclusion, the rules of logic.[24]

While I do not disagree with Sanders' belief that students need to be conscious of the intellectual processes they are employing, I take issue with his statement that this level cannot be used until it is mastered by teachers and pupils. Teachers and students do not have to wait until they have mastered formal logic before they engage in analysis.

Children from grade one upward think. They require opportunities to study, to investigate, to analyze their environment. At this level, children engaging in analysis questions will not be working at a very sophisticated level; nevertheless, they can still be working at the analysis level. To assume that children must wait until they are acquainted with formal logic and rules of reasoning would mean that inquiry cannot exist really in the elementary and perhaps secondary grades. Lacking formal logic students would be inhibited from forming generalizations, which is basic to discovery curricula. Children can work inductively and deductively before they can utter these particular words in the classroom, or even be really conscious of these two strategies of reasoning. Analysis is a crucial part of the discovery curriculum.

[23] Ibid., p. 97.
[24] Ibid., p. 98.

Analysis of Elements

The first sublevel of analysis is *analysis of elements.*[25] These elements may be what is expressed or implied in a written statement or in a person's speech. Or they may be events that have occurred within a period of time. Or they may be landforms that are present in a geographic region. At this level questions can guide an individual in recognizing elements of bias in materials or speeches.

EXAMPLES

1. Study the pictures.
   a. What features of the land appear to be most important to the people who live in this area?
   b. Which occupations appear to be most important?
   c. What principal tools and machines do these people use?
   d. Do the answers to these three questions tell you something about the way of life of these people?
2. Consider the aborigines of Australia. Which of the following assumptions has been made in your text about history in relation to these people?
   a. History is the story of the past, which is passed on by any means, oral or written;
   b. History is understanding the past;
   c. History is having people consider the past;
   d. All of the above statements have been assumed.
3. What are some of the significant elements that explain why black Africans in South Africa who comprise a majority lack the vote in the South African Parliament? Consider the materials you have read and the films you have viewed in preparing your answer to the question.
4. In Mr. Alex's discussion about the myriad political groups in this country, which of his statements are based on facts and which are based on assumptions?
5. Educators are striving to provide schooling for all children in the nation. In the speech given by Mr. Jones, what is his major motive for making the case that he did?

[25] Bloom, *Taxonomy*, pp. 145-46.

Analysis of Relationships

The second level of analysis, *analysis of relationships*, stresses the relationships between various elements recognized.[26] In a written communication the stress is on interrelationships among ideas or major points. Has the writer been consistent in his point of view? How tight are the author's arguments? Are his arguments in line with his major premise? This level of analysis is concerned with the structure of the written communication or with the structure of an environment. A student who has identified the significant elements in his local area may wish to see how these elements interrelate. How does the topographic feature of flatness relate to the major economic activities of the region? How do the social customs of a particular society relate to the behaviors of members of that society? Such questions ask students to analyze the relationships between elements.

EXAMPLES

1. Mr. Smith makes a case in his article for giving the eighteen-year-olds the vote. Analyze his reasoning.
2. Which of the following assumptions is necessary in order to determine the mass of a drop by the method described?
   a. The drop falls with uniform acceleration;
   b. All the drops sprayed into the chamber are of the same size;
   c. The drop is charged;
   d. The drop is nearly spherical;
   e. The electrical force is equal to the gravitational force.[27]
3. Mr. Peters argues that there is a basic inequality between the races. What are some instances of fallacious thinking in his argument?
4. Study the picture showing sheet erosion in the Midwest region. Which of the following was needed in order for this erosion to take place?

26 Ibid., p. 147.
27 Ibid., p. 157. Reprinted by permission.

 a. land contour
 b. poor crop selection
 c. excessive rain
 d. all of the above

Analysis of Organizational Principles

Analysis of organizational principles is the third level of analysis.[28] With regard to written material, this level is concerned with the communication as a whole. What is the overall structure which the author has employed? In literary analysis, questions might be concerned with the way an author has developed his novel. In art, analysis at this level might be concerned with the overall artistic composition that the artist has used to express a particular mood.

Applying analysis to areas other than communication, analysis in geography might center on observing a region, focusing on the profuse interrelationships of topographic features. Also, analysis may require the student to study a particular environment to identify examples of geographic concepts. The student might study the basic chemical structure of certain minerals in the science laboratory. This level will have a great deal more use if we apply it to situations and environments as well as to written or man-made materials.

EXAMPLES

1. From studying the painting of the seascape, can you describe how the artist has used his colors to express the feelings of loneliness and power?
2. Listen to the new symphony. How has the composer developed the piece to give the feeling of contemporary confusion?
3. From listening to the senator's speech, which of the following statements might best describe it?
   a. It was a plea for giving others a chance to voice their opinions;
   b. It argued that dissent without reason is the greatest danger to our country;

[28] Ibid., p. 147.

      c. It made a case for treating dissent in historical perspective;

      d. It called for an overall strengthening of law agencies.

   4. From reading Mr. Jackson's notes on how to develop an effective school, what would you say was his philosophical base?

Synthesis

Synthesis is the fifth level of the taxonomy and requires that students organize the information they have obtained or considered at the lower levels of learning and to produce results based on this study. Bloom mentions that emphasis is upon uniqueness and originality. "In synthesis . . . the student must draw upon elements from many sources and put these together into a structure or pattern not clearly there before."[29]

The student at this level is challenged to draw together the information obtained from his inquiry or discovery or study. What can he say from his analyses? Students confronted with the task of synthesizing must engage to varying degrees the other levels of cognitive functioning. They must have analyzed various situations and applied special skills and knowledge to their quest. Certainly they need to comprehend numerous types of materials and draw from several data bases. Students working at this level do not necessarily proceed orderly through these cognitive stages but rather "jump" back and forth in this hierarchy.

Bloom has divided synthesis into three levels or subcategories: production of a unique communication, production of a plan or proposed set of operations, and derivation of a set of abstract relations.[30]

Production of a Unique Communication

The first requires that the student originate a product that produces ideas, feelings, and experiences uniquely his. This does

[29] Ibid., p. 162.
[30] Ibid., pp. 168-72.

not mean that pure creativity is required of the student. But it does mean that the particular interpretation or slant of the communication or interpretation should represent the student's individual thinking and personality. There are no precise prescriptions as to what the communications must look like. The student has freedom to produce "his own thing."

This intellectual skill of synthesis should be dominant in literature classes or creative-writing classes when students write essays or themes. It can be part of classes in which students make speeches relating to distinct events or ideas.

EXAMPLES

1. Write a paper presenting your interpretation of the current social scene. In the paper you should deal with what you consider the traditional and emergent social values.
2. Write a short story.
3. Write a sonnet.
4. Work together as a group and develop a script for a skit showing the first Thanksgiving.

Production of a Plan

The *production of a plan* requires students to produce a plan or solution to particular situations.[31] Students in the discovery curriculum should be given opportunities to actively engage in working with data. We need to allow students to suggest, from their analyses of various situations, ways in which they will gain additional data or solve particular problems. If students have tentative theories or conclusions, questions at this level can assist them in developing a scheme for testing out the theories.

Our own planning should be an example of this level. After we analyze our students and our facilities, we are faced with the task of developing a plan, either lesson or unit, to meet the needs of students. This plan should represent our in-

[31] Ibid., p. 170.

dividual thinking. It should not merely copy a plan we saw in a methods book.

EXAMPLES

1. Southern California is experiencing problems caused by oil escaping from undersea wells. Study topographic maps and charts of the area and devise a plan that will prevent future leakage.
2. The desert area of southwest Africa is rather fertile but lacks sufficient water for growing crops. Devise a plan to irrigate the region.
3. Consider the social disorders of the present time. In light of the materials studied in class, offer two proposals that would serve to lessen the current tensions.
4. Design a sand table so that you can study the effects of various types of erosion.

These two levels of synthesis are the only two in the taxonomy that cannot be written in multiple-choice format. It is impossible to write options and have the questions unique to the individual's thinking.

Derivation of a Set of Abstract Relations

Derivation of a set of abstract relations comprises the third sub-category of synthesis.[32] This level requires students to create or derive from data or situations analyzed some type of statement to explain or classify the data. In other words, this level means that students can formulate a concept or generalization from the analysis of data.

In the discovery curriculum, this is a crucial, if not the most crucial, activity. The discovery curriculum allows students to deal with data, situations, and different environments, in order to conceptualize and generalize. What statements can the student make from his study of a particular situation that will be applicable to other situations?

[32] Ibid., p. 171.

Questions at this level can also challenge students to develop hypotheses from their previous analyses. Perhaps a student's goal is to develop a theory from his investigation. The central focus of Suchman's inquiry is that students construct theories or hypotheses and then formulate ways to check them out. These two tasks represent levels three and two respectively of the synthesis category. If this level of functioning is central to the current stress on discovery curriculum and active learning, we need more questions and challenges to students at this level.

EXAMPLES

1. A housing concern has made some experiments on methods of heating houses. A room was constructed with walls that could be heated or refrigerated at the same time that air of any temperature was being circulated through the room. Several individuals were asked to record their sensations as the conditions were varied as follows:

	Wall Temp.	*Air Temp.*	*Sensations*
1	85°	85°	uncomfortably hot
2	85°	50°	uncomfortably hot
3	70°	85°	comfortable
4	70°	70°	comfortable
5	70°	50°	comfortable
6	50°	50°	very cold
7	50°	85°	cold

How can you explain the sensation of "coldness" by a person in a room where the air temperature is 85° and the wall temperature is 50°?[33]

2. Mr. Jones states that he has no prejudices. He advocates that minorities be given opportunities equal to those of others. A few months after he makes this statement, a black family moves into Mr. Jones's neighborhood. Mr. Jones is greatly disturbed by this and begins to think of moving to another neighborhood. How can you explain Mr. Jones's behavior?

[33] Ibid., p. 184. Reprinted by permission.

3. Study the political situations in these three countries. What are two statements that would explain the existing phenomena?

4. Consider how we use language in our classroom and how it is used in the outside community. What general statement can you give that would explain the role of language in man's society?

Evaluation

Evaluation is the taxonomy's last category. However, Bloom makes the point and I concur that evaluation is not an activity done after all the other levels of intellectual skills have been used. To some degree evaluation can be considered a "floating" category in that it is or can be used at each level of intellectual activity. The student in dealing with specific facts needs to ascertain if the data have relevance to his search. He needs to evaluate the effectiveness of his comprehension or the effectiveness with which he applies certain understandings and skills. He needs to apply it to the conclusions resulting from his analysis and synthesis.

Evaluation is defined by Bloom "as the making of judgments about the value, for some purpose, of ideas, works, solutions, methods, materials, etc. It involves the use of criteria as well as standards for appraising the extent to which particulars are accurate, effective, economical, or satisfying."[34] Evaluation is crucial in the discovery curriculum in both the inductive and the deductive aspects. In dealing with situations in an inductive manner, evaluation needs to be used throughout the process to afford the investigator some idea as to the worth of the material encountered and the conclusions drawn. In dealing deductively with materials and situations in the discovery curriculum, the student must evaluate in order to see how well the criteria of a particular concept or generalization apply to other situations or facts with which he is dealing. According to the taxonomy, evaluative judgments can be made in terms of internal evidence and external criteria.

[34] Ibid., p. 185.

Evaluation in Terms of Internal Evidence

Evaluation in terms of internal evidence requires the student to analyze data or conclusions from standpoints such as logical accuracy, consistency, and other internal criteria.[35] Has the author been logical in the development of his argument? Have I been consistent in my techniques of researching this topic? Have the generalizations which I have formulated been consistent with the supporting data? Is the painting a quality work of art by the rules of color composition? These are the types of questions of this level.

EXAMPLES

1. Consider the argument that the author gives for an extended school year. Has he used effective logic in making his case?
2. Assuming that the author has used reliable sources of data for the development of his argument, which of the following statements would most effectively describe this short story?
   a. Strong legislation is needed to regulate the activities of large industries;
   b. The federal government does not have the right to exert great powers over private industry;
   c. The public has the obligation to see that industry does not violate the rights of the general community;
   d. More data would be required before one could answer with any great precision.

Evaluation in Terms of External Criteria

The second subcategory of evaluation is *in terms of judgments by external criteria*.[36] The prime focus is on having the student apply known criteria to judge various situations or conclusions that he encounters or develops. If the student is to judge the effectiveness of a painting, he can use the criteria that a noted group of artists has developed. If he is to evaluate the ap-

[35] Ibid., p. 188.
[36] Ibid., p. 190.

propriateness of certain protest actions, he can employ criteria developed for protest meetings. If he is to determine the effectiveness of a person's speech, he can involve criteria developed in speech class for judging a good speech. He can judge the effectiveness of solutions to urban traffic problems against criteria developed by the department of transportation or a local automobile club.

Criteria can be used to judge every aspect of a student's experience. He can use criteria to judge the effectiveness of theories, of concepts, of various processes, of various conclusions made by himself or others. He can apply criteria as to how effectively man is using his technological knowledge. In a curriculum where the student assumes an active role, he must experience questions that force him to apply criteria to evaluate the experiences and conclusions of himself and others. This should be done as the student works at the several levels. It must be done when the student has concluded his investigation or reaction to another's investigation. Sometimes a student faced with evaluating a particular situation discovers that he has need for further analysis or further comprehension. Evaluation allows the student to have a clear idea as to his present state of knowledge and suggests directions for further study.

EXAMPLES

1. Consider the agricultural developments in the Yakima Valley. Do you think that the farmers of the region are making effective use of its resources?
2. Considering the interracial problems in the United States, how would you rank our solutions to date?
3. In your opinion, how effective has legislation been in ending segregation in the United States?
4. From what we have read in our text on population control, how would you rank the significance of the speakers' points on this problem? Explain your answer.
5. How effective has your method of research been in supplying you with needed data?

SUMMARY

This chapter presented an abbreviated outline of Bloom's Taxonomy. The cognitive levels of knowledge, comprehension, application, analysis, synthesis, and evaluation have been discussed. The main characteristics of types of question directed to each of these levels were considered. Examples were presented. It should be apparent that questions necessitate careful planning; they are not simply groupings of words with question marks. Consideration also was given to the rationale for using various types of questions. Analysis questions can be used in the lower grades and can relate to environment as well as to written or spoken materials. Synthesis questions have a crucial value because at this level concepts and generalizations are formed. In a curriculum emphasizing discovery, teachers should ask sufficient numbers of synthesis questions. Evaluation questions represent a somewhat "floating" category. Students use evaluation in determining the effectiveness or worth of their activities or data at the other taxonomy levels.

3

Formulating
Effective Questions

How can we use knowledge about the types of questions to improve our teaching? How can we get our students involved in asking effective questions?

BECOME KNOWLEDGEABLE

The first step in formulating effective questions is to become knowledgeable about the types of questions. Because we tend to overlook the obvious, one reason that our questions may not be as effective as they might is because we may have assumed a knowledge about questions that we really did not possess.

ANALYZE

The next step is to analyze the educational situation within which we find ourselves. Part of this analysis centers on the student. What is the student's background, his readiness for particular types of learning? What are his interests, both present and potential? Knowledge of the student is central to planning what types of questions to use with particular students. Some means of acquiring this knowledge are by observing the student in class, analyzing his anecdotal records, and by his test scores. The reader must know many other ways by which to obtain information on students.

Another dimension of analysis studies the situation within which one is to conduct a lesson. What are the particular times or teaching arrangements within which the lesson will be taught? What facilities does one have at his disposal? The situation may involve team teaching that could allow a certain type of question planning. Or the situation may refer to individualized study or pupil team learning or large group instruction or working with programmed materials or field trips. Will the situation allow for certain types of questions to be used effectively? If we wish to use questions of analysis we will have to provide adequate time for dealing with such questions. If the situation only allows for a three-minute response to a question, then we, as a rule of thumb, might as well not plan to use analysis questions. Such questions demand more time for student response.

The educational environment affects our educational activities. While our actions and questions are not completely influenced by our surroundings, we must consider the facilities within which we are to work. Educational materials also exist as part of the educational arena. If we wish to ask questions stressing synthesis, specifically formulating a generalization, the educational situation must enable students to discuss, or to consult resource materials, or view filmstrips or meet with the teacher, or view maps and charts. The educational environment cannot be a sterile room with one map, a basic text, and chairs arranged in a row for total class discussion. This sort of environment is not likely to stimulate students to effectively engage in synthesis. Questions can challenge and direct students' activities, but the environment can facilitate or retard the success with which a student meets the challenge of questions.

CONSIDER GOALS AND OBJECTIVES

This step closely relates to the previous one. It may even be done at the same time. After we have come to know our students and their needs and interests and have defined our teaching situation and the facilities, we need to ask ourselves what are the basic goals of our school, or of education in general. We can then see if the information gained in the previous step relates well to the overall aims of the school. If one school's aim is to foster independent thinkers, which would be an aim of the discovery curriculum, we need to ascertain if the students indicate a readiness for such a goal. If not, we need to structure lesson activities, materials, and questions that would develop readiness. Once this is done we can plan strategies to extend pupils' competence as independent thinkers.

Consideration of goals, which are long-range phenomena, is crucial for overall direction to our teaching, our questioning. The discovery curriculum cannot effectively function without such goals. Some of these goals have been implied previously: independent learner, process-oriented learner, active learner, a humanistic learner, an appreciative man. It is evident these goals overlap. Goals should not only suggest definite end products, they should also allow for the unexpected, the different. Those of us concerned with discovery curriculum need to realize that we should be more concerned with beginnings rather than endings. In the discovery-curriculum we want our questions to spur students to active search; we wish our questions to encourage students to begin to understand their world. We need to know direction, but we don't wish to become narrow in looking at the school's goals. A discovery curriculum should foster diversity, not undue conformity among the students.

Once goals have been defined in somewhat flexible terms, we can then consider objectives. Again we need to think of objectives as guides which will need continual alteration to meet the unique needs of persons in the discovery curriculum. Objectives need to be identified and put in behavioral terms to assist us in our evaluation. However, objectives also need to consider the vague, the unplanned, the creative reaction. Objectives to cover these dimensions of discovery curriculum are rather difficult. We do not wish to limit students' learning in attempts to have them all behave in predictable ways. We need balance between objectives behaviorally stated and objectives which can be more open ended.

In considering goals and objectives we need to plan questions that will facilitate student attainment of the said goals or objectives or point the students in the designated directions. For students to analyze data independently they will need questions at the analysis level. We will need to schedule time for the student to dig, to analyze. Often we give lip service to having students analyze and then provide them with questions that only demand comprehension.

Questions are not asked solely to check if students remember what we presented the previous day. Questions should be handles that students apply to gain better grips upon information, upon understanding reality. The objectives we plan should reflect this "handle" use of questions. Objectives should guide the planning and selection of questions.

CONSIDER QUESTION TYPES

What type or types of questions can I formulate to achieve the objectives, the aims of both the school and the student? Here we use Bloom's Taxonomy as a guide or some other guide and check question examples. How do the questions I have tentatively planned compare with the examples presented? Are they worded so that students will be capable of responding to them? Are we considering the types of questions needed to fit the objectives and overall lessons planned? If our objective is to have students comprehend certain written materials, then we need to be sure that comprehension questions are placed crucially in the lesson's planned sequence. If our objective is student formulation of generalizations (synthesis), then our questions need to be at this level. We need to continually check tentative questions against some type of guide, at least initially, when dealing with questions.

Not only must we consider question types, we must consider the effects, potential effects, that certain types of questions will have on students. The effects can relate to both the cognitive and affective domain. Will the question as you have worded it really cause the particular student to analyze a particular situation? Or will such a question, if asked at this time, produce frustration with his performing the task? Knowing the effects that certain questions will elicit can allow· us to plan with some precision the total learning situation. It will allow us to anticipate various reaction avenues.

CRITERIA

In considering question types, we also need to think about criteria for selecting content and experiences. The content should relate to the achievement of objectives; it needs to be supportive of higher order abstractions; it needs a high interest potential; it should be relevant to the student's needs; it requires necessary support materials; it needs to be feasible in terms of cost, time required to learn, and ease of implementation.

When working with formulating questions, we need to keep such criteria in mind. The questions we plan are vital elements of the content. They must assist in the achievement of objectives; they need to facilitate the development of higher order abstractions, concepts, and generalizations. The questions, if they are to effectively stimulate pupils to various levels of cognition, will require adequate materials for effective student reaction to questions. Questions require time. When we plan questions, we need to ask if the questions we are asking are feasible in terms of the time scheduled. If we have twenty minutes, we are not likely to be able to engage pupils in reacting to high-level questions. However, it is possible to ask high-level questions on one day and not expect a response until the end of the week. We need to get away from the practice of expecting an answer to all our questions three minutes or less after we ask them.

Criteria for effective questions not only relate to the criteria for selecting content and activities. We should also use criteria specifically relating to forming the questions. Perhaps the first criterion for an effective question relates to its wording. Does the question's wording make clear what it expects, both cognitively and affectively, from the student? Can the student understand what the question means? Remember that a question's wording can be misleading from a cognitive standpoint. All questions beginning with "How" and "Why" are not high-level questions. Therefore the wording of the question should be done in relation to the pupil's prior experience and the current class situation. Does the wording of a question allow the student to respond with optimal productivity? Does the wording of the question provide the student with adequate directions for the task? Does the question's wording provide unnecessary clues for the student? Does the question's wording allow the student to see the relationship of this particular question with ones previously asked? Of course, if the question is one of numerous objective types, such as multiple choice, matching, completion, the rules for such construction should be followed. Rather than go into detail as to how to write these various "mechanical" types, I would recommend one review a tests and measurement text. I would like to stress, however, that knowing how to write a multiple choice question with discriminating options does not mean that one can write a high-level question. Multiple choice questions can be at the knowledge level, or they can be at the synthesis or evaluation levels.

A question such as "react to the situation" may not be very effective in that the student has inadequate information as to how to proceed or exactly what the task is. A tighter phrasing is, Comparing the two situations, what are the major commonalities? Or, Considering the information, what are some conclusions you can formulate? These questions are still somewhat general, but the student does realize that he has to end with some conclusions.

How much information to provide the student in the wording of the question depends upon the particular learning situation and what cognitive level you wish to emphasize. Usually, the more clues in the wording as to what the student is to do the lower is the cognitive level. Perhaps when dealing with the writing of questions, a prime criterion is that of clearness. Does the wording facilitate effective student functioning? If the question is to stimulate analysis and the student misinterprets and just regurgitates information, then the question needs revision or it needs to be planned for another lesson sequence.

WRITE OR SELECT THE QUESTIONS

After considering the various types of questions and their potential effects, we are ready to either write or select them. Usually, in our plans, we write some tentative questions. These guide our thinking as we develop a lesson to involve the students. Here we need to consider the ideal and the actual cognitive emphasis. Perhaps we can develop a scheme such as the following:

IDEAL	ACTUAL
What is the name of the river in this region? (*Knowledge*)	
Compare the two forms of government in this region. (*Comprehension*)	The actual emphasis cannot be determined until after the questioning session.
Are the Arab nations making effective use of their natural resources? (*Evaluation*)	

You will recall that mention was made of heuristic questions. These are the crucial questions planned to either guide or stimulate the student to deal with the discovery curriculum.

These are the questions that we are planning primarily. These are the questions listed in the ideal column. We will have to wait until after the lesson to determine the actual emphasis.

When writing questions we should exert care that our intended emphasis is reflected in the wording. We need to ascertain that the questions have some interest level. We should try to vary the wording. Similarly worded questions make for boring listening and can tend to turn off students. We teachers should experiment with myriad ways of writing questions at the separate cognitive levels. For example, if we are asking an evaluation question, we should not always begin with, Evaluate the effectiveness of. . . . Perhaps we might begin with, Which conclusion is most justified . . . ? The examples given in the previous chapter may offer assistance in achieving variety in question wording.

Usually the questions we write in our plans are samples of questions that we will use in our lessons. But many of the questions will be taken from diverse materials and books. We need to study such materials to check the questions included. Are the questions effective in relation to our lesson's objectives? Can the questions in the text stimulate interest with these students? Can my students deal wih these questions productively? Do I have adequate time to deal with the questions in the text? Are the questions in the materials of comparable cognitive emphasis with those used in class dialogue? Are the text questions so sequenced as to complement the questioning strategy that I am using?

Often upon analyzing the questions in textbooks, we find a dominance of one type of question and this type may be of low order. If so, then in planning we need to revise the questions to reflect the cognitive emphasis of the class. If a section of the text contains mostly knowledge questions, we may wish to develop analysis questions taking the cues from the knowledge questions. In the discovery curriculum, we should refrain from the technique of having students merely read the text and respond to the questions at the end of a section.

If necessary, the questions should be revised so that they

facilitate the achievement of stated objectives and relate to the readiness and interests of the pupils. Again, time schedule must be considered. Do the revised questions meet the relevancy criterion? Are the revisions clearly worded without giving undue clues to the answers? Do they reflect the intended cognitive level? Such considerations must be made when selecting questions from texts, articles, games, or the curriculum guide.

Many of the new curriculum projects incorporate excellent sample questions. But we should not assume that all the questions are appropriate to our particular students. We need to determine the cognitive levels emphasized. We need to check these levels in relation to our own classes. Often we must upgrade the questions in such materials because of the backgrounds of our students. At other times we will have to adjust the cognitive levels downward because of particular needs.

JUDGE THE QUESTIONS

Once we have our tentative questions either written or selected we should, at least at first, have someone judge them. Of course, the judge should know the types of questions. He can be one of our colleagues. The judging of questions is most profitable if you and your judge work together. This allows discussion of the situations in which the questions will be employed. A judge working alone might rank a question at one level, while in discussing it with you he might see the total planned experience and rank the question differently. Isolated questions are difficult to judge.

Those questions that the judge seriously questions should be at least rethought and quite likely rewritten. If a judge is not too sure of how to respond to a question, a student may also find difficulty. We in team-teaching arrangements have ideal situations for joint preparation, selection, and judging of questions.

Judges not only can rank the questions we formulate, but they can assist us in determining just how effectively the questions fit into planned reaction avenues. A colleague can assist us to determine the probability of a particular reaction avenue materializing in response to particular questions. Perhaps we might have some unproductive questions or ones that are not essential to the development of a particular path of discovery.

Judges not only can react to our questions as to their wording and potential productiveness in the discovery curriculum, they can also assist us in judging and planning materials and experiences to provide in dealing with particular questions. If we have a question asking pupils to formulate a generalization about human behavior in group situations, a colleague may assist us in pointing out particular materials beneficial for student reaction to the question. Perhaps we have the question, What are the significant factors that led to the location of this shopping center? This is an analysis question in which the student must identify significant elements of geography and economics in the environment. A judge might know of some primary resources that could help the children form an answer. Or he may be able to indicate a particular simulation game which can help students answer questions relating to concepts of economic location. Or the judge may say that the question is unrealistic in terms of the number of class meetings scheduled.

Having a person react to our questions should not be viewed as threatening. Developing effective questions is complex. It takes time. Colleague cooperation provides mutual benefit; sometime we may be asked to serve as a judge to his questions and planning. The discovery curriculum requires greater cooperation among teachers.

Judges can react to our overall questioning strategies as well as to particular questions. A question needs to be planned in relation to other questions. The reaction avenue discussed previously can be considered as a potential questioning strategy. The questioning strategy of Bloom's Taxonomy proceeds from an emphasis upon knowledge questions and works toward the higher cognitive levels. Judges can study our overall questioning plan and decide whether it will achieve the objectives of the lesson. Will it involve the students in activity dealing with data? This is a question that should often be asked in the discovery curriculum.

GETTING STUDENTS TO FORMULATE EFFECTIVE QUESTIONS

The central factor of the discovery curriculum is the student's participation in the process of learning. For students to be active they must be knowledgeable about questions and how to use them effectively. One of our goals related to the process domain should be to make students effective questioners.

An atmosphere for facilitating learning is basic for enabling students to be good questioners. Such an atmosphere allows students time for reaction and provides necessary materials. Such an atmosphere schedules time to really dig into a question response. It does not require an answer to a question in the next minute or before the bell rings. An atmosphere that facilitates inquiry makes students responsible for much of their own learning. The teacher guides rather than tells much of the time. Students are encouraged to investigate their own methods of study. The teacher allows diversity of approaches to inquiry depending upon needs, interests, and topic. In such an environment the teacher provides encouragement, not pressure to respond without careful thought or sufficient investigation.

Allowing Students to Gain Insights

Students, to be effective inquirers, must have opportunities to see the question used as an effective tool. As teachers we must be careful that we are good exemplars. Do we use questions to stimulate pupils in their search? Do we use questions as handles to attain understanding in greater depth?

For students to become proficient in asking questions requires time. Sufficient time should be scheduled into the discovery curriculum sequence. Time must be provided for you to ask challenging questions. Time must be provided for students to ask questions of you and their classmates. Students require opportunities to raise questions needing investigation. Let students react to various data and then list questions that they deem significant. Then let them discuss their selection with their peers. Explaining why these questions are crucial may be more useful in the learning process than the actual answers to which the questions guide pupils. Such dialogue requires students to ask themselves just what information they are seeking. What value does it have for them?

Students should have opportunity to formulate criteria for good questions. One criterion could be that the question should advance one's specific state of knowledge. Another could be that the question should lead one to understand more fully the overall problem being studied. Another might be that the question should guide one's thinking in drawing a warranted conclusion. Additionally, a question should stimulate precision of one's cognitive process.

These criteria differ somewhat from those previously stated since they do not just relate to the general construction of the question. Rather, these criteria consider questions in relation to a particular student or teacher goal. Of course, some of the more general criteria relating to wording and ideal cognitive emphasis also should be tied in with these specific criteria. A student should ask himself what he wants his questions to do for him. Does he want information? Does the question he has raised obtain it? Does he want to check out the structure of this composition? Does the question he has formulated direct him to this particular goal?

Formal Discussion of Questions

Students can learn a great deal about questions and their effective use from just being allowed opportunities to formulate some and carry out investigations of them. However, informal learning about questions should not exclude formal instruction. Students can have periods of time designated for focusing on their processes of inquiry or problem-solving. Such focus would naturally deal with questions. Here students can analyze the types of questions they have been asking. Are they satisfied with their questions? Have they considered their questions productive in directing them to designated goals? What is the type of question they most commonly formulate?

Students presented opportunities to inquire within the discovery curriculum will most likely develop felt needs for formal discussion of questions. Students who are active in learning need to have time scheduled for analyzing just how they proceed. We can discuss with students the several types of questions according to some guide such as Bloom. We should be sure that it is a guided discussion rather than just an exposition. We can present for discussion the idea that various types of questions will provide certain types of data. We might direct consideration as to what students do in questioning when they wish to formulate a generalization.

Before commencing formal discussion of questions, the teacher assigns students the task of listing some of the major questions they used in dealing with particular research topics. This list can then be considered in class group discussion. Students can analyze and criticize the different questions listed. Such activity could serve as a focus for considering question types. Just what are the characteristics of the many questions asked? Why do you suppose this question was asked? If a student wished to develop a generalization, should he have asked primarily comprehension questions?

Such focus on questions also can lead to a consideration of the numerous questioning strategies students used. Students engaged in oral investigation with a team partner might record their questions as they consider data. The tapes could then be studied to check if certain types of questions were used at the beginning of the inquiry and other types at the end. Where did the student put his most significant questions in relation to his search? Did he comprise a list of significant questions to search for, or did he just react to specific types of data and then draw questions from this experience?

Related to student consideration of questioning strategies is emphasis upon cognitive mapping. We can tape a particular class lesson and then develop a cognitive map of the session. We can analyze the directions the session took and can identify the major questions that focused and redirected our investigating. One would not do this every week, but it could be done at specified intervals, perhaps once a month. With such regular consideration, students could see their improvement in questions asked and strategies employed as the year progressed.

Students also should have time for practicing writing various types of questions and for judging the questions of others. Students can be grouped in teams of two and use each other as sounding boards regarding their questions. Perhaps the class can develop certain guides in formulating the several types of questions. The development of criteria for effective questions can be a class task. Here students could do some reading on the question and its importance. Students could read about inquiry in articles published in school magazines.

Related to writing diverse questions is being able to identify questions in written materials. Students, perhaps in teams, can analyze questions in textbooks and various supplementary books. Such analysis could focus on the intent of the questions. Also, if students wished to gain information other than that asked for in the material, what types of questions would they have to state?

Awareness of Process

To become a truly independent learner the student needs detailed knowledge of process. We can start in the early grades to develop this knowledge. This awareness will develop from not only asking the student what he knows, but from asking him how he got to know what he knows. Students also must query themselves as to what processes they did employ. Were these the most productive processes possible? If he had asked other questions, would he have reached a different conclusion, or the same conclusion sooner?

In such situations the student is inquiring into process. Students as they progress through the grades will perfect their understandings. They will be well equipped to be autonomous learners if we structure such formal dealings with process and with related questions.

Awareness of process can facilitate the student in developing an aggressive attitude toward learning and an eagerness to understand his world. This is a crucial goal of the discovery curriculum. Students with this attitude also develop a way of accepting many of their present conclusions on a tentative basis. Students realize that they should not terminate their searches for additional data. Learning is not completed even in an area that the student knows well; it is ongoing. There will always be questions that can be posed regarding today's conclusions.

Summary

This chapter dealt with the steps to use in formulating effective questions. The first step, after becoming informed about questions, is to analyze our students, the facilities, the materials, and the time schedule we have. The second step is to consider the goals of the school and then how to meet them. After that, we consider question types. What types of questions will assist students to achieve the objectives chosen? The effects of questions on students must be considered. The teacher develops questions for use in the particular lesson paying attention to the ideal and actual emphasis of questions. The teacher can get questions from textbooks, from guides, from various projects, and from his own creativity. After selecting questions, the teacher should ask colleagues to react to and judge his questions. Are the questions appropriate for the intended levels? The judge can also evaluate reaction avenues. Potential materials, environments, and experiences which would help students in the learning process are weighed.

Getting students to formulate good questions was emphasized. The main objective is to allow students to become independent in learning by teaching them process and the place of questions in process. The teacher needs to develop an atmosphere which stresses the need to ask questions and should provide situations and adequate time for students to pose questions.

Students need insights into the realm of questions. The teacher should be an exemplar of the good questioner. Students need opportunities to formulate and to react to their own questions either alone or with a teammate or in a large group. Formal instruction in questions and questioning is a means of making the student cognizant of questions. Such formal instruction can focus on the types of questions, the functions of questions, and the various types of strategies. Finally students in the discovery curriculum need time to inquire into their data gathering processes. Such consideration not only gives students understanding of process but a positive attitude toward themselves, their learning, their environment.

4

Questioning
Strategies

Questions do not exist in isolation. They exist within a scheme
which is either planned or assumed. This chapter focuses on
some strategies to enable us to incorporate a particular questioning procedure into our teaching. Since research on questioning methods is sparse and results conflicting, I will present
several specific and implied questioning strategies.

FUNCTIONS OF QUESTIONS AND
QUESTIONING STRATEGIES

Before discussing various questioning plans we should consider
the functions of questions when grouped within a particular
scheme. In a previous chapter the cognitive functions of
questions were discussed in view of Bloom's taxonomy: the
recall of knowledge, the comprehension of material, the application of knowledge and skills, the analysis of situations or
materials, the synthesis of various types of data, and the
evaluation of the results of inquiry. But questions are not asked
in isolation; they comprise elements of questioning strategies.

Questions incorporated into strategies can have four possible overall functions: centering, expansion, distribution,
ordering. The first two, centering and expansion, are guiding

functions by which the teacher assists students to either focus on material at a particular cognitive level or to engage in divergent thinking at a particular cognitive level or to raise their investigation or reaction to another cognitive level. The distribution function is a management function aimed at involving students in their learning. The fourth function, ordering, relates to classroom control and maintaining an environment conducive to productive student learning.

Centering Function

The centering function of a question strategy strives to converge students' thinking on a particular topic or aspect of a topic. Centering is usually employed in the introductory stage of a lesson when we are attempting to get students to attend to the topic of study. Suchman[1] suggests that a discrepant event be provided as a focus for centering attention. Centering also is used in the development of a lesson when we wish to have the students collect information gathered and focus on a particular aspect of it. Perhaps we have been urging students to think of ways in which to eliminate smog. Students have responded with numerous solutions. Now we incorporate a series of questions, which can be at different cognitive levels, to guide students to isolate the more powerful suggestions and to converge on those most warranted. The centering function attempts to channel the consideration of many ideas or situations into the consideration of a few major ideas or significant situations.

In using a questioning scheme emphasizing the centering function, we could provide our students with clues as to the productiveness of their search. We might even provide information or answers to assist them in focusing and consolidating their ideas. It should be remembered that the discovery

---

[1] Suchman's inquiry is discussed later in this text. In his strategy he urges the teacher to provide a focus for inquiry either through a film, picture, or statement that evidences what appears to be a discrepant event: e.g., water boiling on a cake of ice.

in the classroom is not the pure discovery of scholars. Rather, it is a guided discovery in which we assist students to arrive at various important perceptions and facts. We may use questions in such a method to provide support for pupils in their working with data.

A questioning procedure stressing this centering function also may ask students to formulate questions to identify new foci.

NOTE: The solid lines represent the questions asked to get from prior situation to focus to conclusion.

Figure 4.1. Diagram of a questioning strategy emphasizing the centering function

Figure 4.1 indicates both an inductive and deductive mode of operation. It is inductive if the prior situation is a specific instance from which one is to generalize. It is deductive if the prior situation represents a generalized situation or statement which is being applied or centered to a specific situation or fact. Perhaps some of the questions the teacher uses are clues to jog students' memories as to what was learned previously or to guide them to apply a generalization to the particular situation to check the validity of the situation, or at least to test the validity of their interpretation of the situation.

In the centering function of a question strategy the teacher attempts to direct students to actively formulate questions for investigation. Questions encouraging students to share the planning of an investigation fall under the centering function.

The center function can involve all the Taxonomy's levels. However, questions at the specific cognitive levels are used to direct the grouping of information into meaningful combinations so that a focus or a limited number of foci result. In the centering function, the teacher provides direction as to what process to apply and what data to consider significant.

The various functions of questioning schemes do not exist in precise categories. Rather the function is the directional push or emphasis of the grouping of questions. Certainly, in dealing with discovery curriculum, we and the students will use a blend of functions. Let us consider an example:

Mr. Jackson wishes to have his students become familiar with some of the major social issues confronting cities today. He decides to employ a strategy with a centering function to direct his students' attention to two or three issues for class study. He begins the lesson by posing some knowledge questions such as the following: What is a definition of a city? What is a definition of a social issue? What current social problem needs solution? He then brings in some comprehension questions such as, What social issues does our text consider? How would you interpret the author's statement regarding social issues needing attention? Some application questions also aimed at centering the inquiry follow: Look at these three movies of happenings in American cities. What theories regarding urban problems can be applied to these situations? Look at the map on page 5 showing population distribution in cities A and B and suggest reasons why conflicts developed in these cities during the last two years.

Once students have responded to some of these questions and raised others, they begin to sift information for importance and relevance. Perhaps the students list the three events receiving the major emphasis in the investigation. The teacher provides hints as the students react: Is the material going to provide data with which you can work? Does everyone in the class agree with the findings of this group? This is asking for a type of evaluation. However, you will recall that evaluation was described as a "floating" category. After some consideration of these questions, the students should have centered on the major social issues currently confronting cities.

Expansion Function

Expansion, the second questioning strategy function, guides students to expand or extend their thinking. It can exist at the same cognitive level stressing depth, or it can aim at raising the cognitive level of the students' reactions to information. Taba,[2] in discussing questions, identified two functions of questions that would be similar to this expansion function, the extension of thought at the same level and the lifting of thought to another level.

Question strategies emphasizing expansion stress divergent thinking. If students are working at the comprehension level, the strategy can guide them to extrapolate information. At the application stage, the strategy can direct them to produce several conclusions or apply particular skills to wider situations. The expansion function requires increased student precision and greater student involvement in investigation. The expansion function often emphasizes the higher cognitive levels. Students are guided to analyze data not only to identify elements and relationships but to apply information learned in one situation to other situations.

Let us consider the expansion function at the analysis cognitive level. Suppose that the lesson's objective is for stu-

[2] Hilda Taba, *Teachers' Handbook for Elementary Social Studies*, intro ed. (Reading, Mass.: Addison-Wesley Publishing Co., 1967), pp. 121, 122.

dents to identify significant social relationships that influence international dealings. The questions framed guide students in searching for significant elements of social interaction. Questions accentuate divergence of thought as well as divergence of process and material use. The teacher poses questions such as, If these are three significant factors in determining successful social interaction, what additional factors could influence such behavior? Indicate other sources we could utilize in our search. Is there another way of looking at this material? Do we have any conflicting reactions to the tentative factors already identified?

The teacher is posing questions to get students to consider information from varying stances and to keep them from prematurely converging on particular information. Students are to look for other possibilities. Still the stress is on analysis. When such analysis has revealed significant elements or factors, the questioning strategy can still function at the analysis level and work for expansion to analysis of relationships. What are some of the relationships evidenced? Can we find relationships dominating the various groupings of data presently gathered? Is there any consistency of results when we employ these sets of relationships to explain the particular problem under study?

Once students have, through divergent thinking, discovered several significant factors and significant relations, the teacher might use questions to engage students at higher cognitive levels. The expansion function also can lower the cognitive considerations of students. This might occur if the class were experiencing difficulty in working at a particular cognitive level and needed information at the comprehension level. In such a move, the questioning strategy might shift from expansion to centering, although one can have expansion at the lower cognitive levels providing one is continually stressing divergence of answers. The matter of stress is crucial to understand in order to ascertain whether a strategy has a centering or an expansion function.

However, let us assume that the teacher is expanding class action to a higher cognitive level. Perhaps students are trying to formulate some generalizations regarding international dealings. Here the teacher employs synthesis questions, primarily stressing the derivation of abstract relationships, or the forming of a generalization or generalizations. The teacher guides pupils in weighing various data. Perhaps emphasis is upon developing several generalizations that would relate to international dealings. However, once students have engaged in divergent thought and produced several conclusions, the strategy might shift to centering in order to draw the most warranted conclusion. Usually such a stress is not dominant since even if the students do center on a particular generalization, the teacher through guided discovery assists students in extending their generalization to other situations. The generalization can serve as a guide in predicting other international situations.

A diagram of the expansion function of a questioning strategy would look like Figure 4.2.

This diagram represents basically the preceding discussion. As indicated, the initial questions stressed students' extending their thinking at the analysis level. The resulting varied conclusions then were used to enable students to function at the synthesis level. In the guided discovery, there was a point where the questions directed the students to center on a particular generalization. However, the generalization selected then was used to expand students' thought to other levels.

Consider this example: Students are studying causes for the prevention of erosion. The teacher provides the class with pictures of areas affected and not affected by erosion. The class also has sand tables for conducting experiments on the effects of various ground covers on water run-off. Books and filmstrips on the subject also are available. The initial questions direct students to extend their thinking about the elements of erosion: Looking at the picture (showing severe gully erosion), what is the condition of the land? What are some factors that might have caused this condition? The stress then shifts to analysis of relationships: What are some relationships that might exist between some of the factors identified,

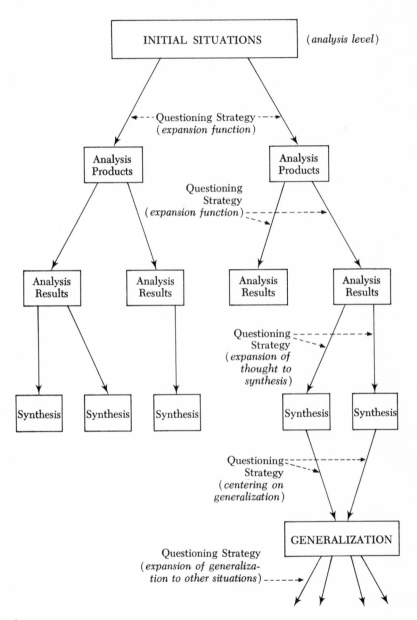

NOTE: The solid lines represent the questions asked to get students to function at various levels.

Figure 4.2. Scheme indicating the expansion function of questions

such as land contour, climate, depth of bed rock, type of soil? In how many ways could such relationships influence the loss of top soil? Stress here is on relationships and expanding the understanding of these relationships to top soil. What are potential uses for this information about the relationship between the various factors of an environment and erosion? Here questions are attempting to raise the cognitive level to synthesis. From our study of these materials and from our field trip in the community, what are some general statements that can be made about erosion? Are these statements applicable to other situations? How? What is the value of knowing this information? These last questions are asking students to think how they can expand their information and to consider the value of such expansion.

These two guiding functions, centering and expansion, are crucial to supporting students in assuming active roles in their learning and for helping them to gain meaning of information encountered. Students, after they acquire understanding of the question and questioning strategies, can use their knowledge to further their self-education.

Distribution Function

This function and the next function, the order function, are closely related in that they both focus on enabling students to engage in or respond to the two guiding functions. However, I consider a difference between distribution, which aims at involving students in working with data, and order, which makes for an atmosphere in which students can be productively involved. Before considering exactly what distribution is, one should realize that the distribution function works along with the centering and expansion function. We may wish to involve many students in converging on data or in working divergently with data.

The distribution function simply allows many students to participate in the class session. It is easy to focus our questions to those students who are always ready with the correct response. However, our questions should trigger thinking, not just correct response. We should consciously involve most if not all students. How one develops distribution can vary. One can distribute questions by acknowledging the raised hands of students. Or one can use nonverbal clues. The important point is that questions are distributed to motivate thinking and to assess present states of knowledge, but not to embarrass students who may not know an answer or who are caught daydreaming.

The distribution of questions is essential when dealing with the expansion function of questioning. Here one is dealing with and looking for questions that have multiple answers or applications. Here different answers to expansion questions should be solicited from many class members. Students need to be involved lest they mentally drop out of the educational experience. Nonparticipating students need encouragement to become involved. In the discovery curriculum, students should be urged to challenge each other's thinking. The distribution of questions can help in reaching this goal.

Order Function

The last questioning strategy function is ordering. This also exists as part of the centering or expansion function. Usually it is not represented by an extended series of questions but by specific questions asked at various times to maintain a classroom atmosphere conducive to the discovery curriculum. Many of these questions would be what Davis and Tinsley[3] call procedure questions. Their procedure category might also take in the distribution function of questions.

The order function is for the purpose of classroom management. Questions having this function ask students rules of class investigation and rules of conduct: When can we work with a teammate? What regulations have we regarding getting out of

---

[3] O. L. Davis, Jr., and Drew C. Tinsley, "Cognitive Objectives Revealed by Classroom Questions Asked by Social Studies Student Teachers," *Peabody Journal of Education*, XLV, no. 1 (July 1967): 21-26.

our seats? leaving the room? When is it permissible to miss a class discovery session? What are some things we must do when engaged in an inquiry session? Sometimes rhetorical questions may be asked under the order function: You really don't mean to say that you will be doing that all day? However, questions such as this should be kept at a minimum.

Questions having the order function can also be related to providing emotional support for students. Often students fail to become actively involved because of feelings of insecurity. Questions can be asked that will offer them encouragement to participate: What are some of the reasons that keep you from participating in discussion? What are some situations you would like to join? avoid? Is there anything that I can do to assist you in participating? What are your feelings about engaging in inquiry? How can I help you in dealing with these data? These questions aim at student support but because some could embarrass a student they most likely should be asked in private conference with the student. These questions provide us with information indicating ways we can work effectively with the student. In guiding the student in working in his environment, we also are contributing to the productive order of the class. The order function of questions is not to inhibit inquiry or discovery or to assure the quiet classroom. It is to order the environment so that students can be effective members of the learning situation.

QUESTIONING STRATEGIES

The previous section considered the types of functions other than cognitive that questioning strategies can assume. This section discusses various questioning methods. The reader should react to these specific strategies not as if one were the best or the right one. Most likely no one strategy would be effective in all situations; it is plausible that several strategies will work in certain types of situations. However, before we can select a technique for use, we must understand the different types. Then we will be able to choose one or perhaps develop a hybrid or a new strategy for our own class.

Bloom's Taxonomy—an Implicit Strategy

Much attention has been given in this text to Bloom's Taxonomy. It was considered in some depth with regard to question types and has been mentioned regarding the functions of questioning procedures relating to their cognitive emphasis. It is inherent that if Bloom's Taxonomy is a taxonomy, the higher categories subsume the lower. This means that the various levels of the taxonomy serve as building blocks. If we have an objective of synthesis for a particular lesson, the student is going to have to be able to function at the lower levels of knowledge, comprehension, application, and analysis. If the student has adequate understanding and skills at these levels, then a questioning strategy could have the function of expansion at the synthesis level for increased depth at this level. However, if students lack requisite skills and knowledge to function at the synthesis level, they would need experiences at the lower cognitive levels. Thus it seems that a scheme as implied by Bloom's Taxonomy is to develop questions that center and expand the activities of students at each level.

For instance, a unit's objective may be to discover the relationship between the standard of living in a country and the level of technology. First, the teacher develops a series of questions designed to center students' attention on the particular problem of understanding the relationship .between standard of living and level of technology. The first class sessions might provide for students to react to questions dealing with specifics, such as the number of people who have televisions in the country. What is the total output of various factories in terms of units produced? What is the average income of people in the United States? Knowledge questions about terminology might be asked: What do we call the device by which manufactured products are moved from start to finish of production? What do we mean by the term "technology"? What is the meaning of "standard of living"?

Questions at the knowledge level might ask students to identify procedures for gaining additional answers to some questions. They could direct students to certain trends and sequences relating to the standard of living: Do people in the United States have more material goods today than they did in 1940? At this centering stage, the students could be asked to identify types of information needed or desired to advance and direct their investigation.

After questions dealing with the knowledge level have centered the students' attention on the problem to be investigated and provided an adequate data base for further inquiry, the teacher can shift to a questioning strategy emphasizing expansion. Here students' cognition would be raised from the level of knowledge to the level of comprehension. Questions such as the following might be used at this stage: What does the book say about the standard of living in the United States? When the author discusses gross national product, what does he mean? Using the information available in our text, how might we graphically illustrate the trend production is taking? What is the central idea of Chapter 3 on this situation? What is the central thought of the speech by the leading economist? If the current situation continues, what can we predict will happen in ten years? These questions are primarily concerned with the expansion function at the comprehension level. Their goal is to enable students to begin comprehending the links between technology and standard of living.

When he feels students have sufficient data, the teacher can use questions, or allow students to develop questions, which are aimed at applying knowledge gained at the knowledge and comprehension levels. He can ask questions such as, Study the map and indicate where one is likely to find a high degree of technology and a high standard of living. Looking at the situation in this part of the country, what solutions could you suggest to enable production to increase? (Here attention is on application of principles of production.) If this part of the country is increasing in population at this particular rate, then how long will it take before the law of diminishing returns will come into action? Again, the prime focus is on expansion. However, at some point in the questioning, the teacher may decide that the students have too much data and are becoming confused. He may then shift to a questioning strategy of centering. Here he would direct the students to apply their knowledge and experiences to group information according to some criterion or principle.

After questions have been utilized to engage students at the application stage, they can be used to direct students to the analytical level. Questions dealing with several elements in the economy and relationships between economic factors of production and standard of living would come into focus: What three conditions are necessary for a particular economic situation to evolve? If this situation exists, what might be some of its effects on this community? At this analysis level, questions may center on the different arguments economists have presented in discussing this particular problem: Has the author presented a strong case for indicating that, without these materials, the level of production will diminish and the standard of living will be adversely affected?

After students have reacted to these analysis questions, synthesis questions aimed at producing both convergent and divergent thinking can be asked. Perhaps questions ask students to converge on the three best solutions to a particular economic problem. Perhaps questions ask them to think of ways to improve the standard of living in a particular area. Finally, the end goal of the guided discovery is to formulate concepts and generalizations to explain the relationships between the level of technology and the standard of living. These questions are at the third level of synthesis, the derivation of a set of abstract relations. At this level questions would be used to center attention on forming a generalization. Once the generalization has been stated, questions might encourage student application of conclusions to as many situations as possible and to obtain an even greater depth of understanding.

Figure 4.3 is a representation of the preceding discussion. As the diagram shows, both centering and expansion questions are used to help students reach increasingly higher levels of learning. Of course, not all questioning episodes would start at the knowledge level. Many would begin at the synthesis level in which information gained previously would be incorporated into the synthesizing activities. The diagram reveals that an overall questioning procedure would have different functions depending upon the specific needs and objectives of the students and the objectives of the teacher.

Taba's Questioning Strategy

Taba[4] discussed the functions of questions as focusing, extending thought at the same level, and lifting thought to another level. She related these functions to questions and not to questioning strategies. Her first function is similar to my centering functioning of a questioning strategy. Her extension of thought and the lifting of thought could be parts of my expansion function.

Taba[5] stated that the sequencing of questions was most often arbitrary. Teachers and students rarely give careful thought to the questions they pose and where they sequence them. Taba did not specifically identify the cognitive stages of questions; rather she ranked them as "What?," "Why?," and "What does it mean?" These questions were tied into three cognitive tasks: Cognitive Task I: Concept Formation;[6] Cognitive Task II: Interpretation of Data;[7] and Cognitive Task III: Application of Principles.[8] At each of these task levels, pupils would be asked questions starting with "What?" and

[4] Taba, op. cit., pp. 119-22.

[5] Ibid., p. 123.

[6] Ibid., p. 91.

[7] Ibid., p. 101.

[8] Ibid., p. 109.

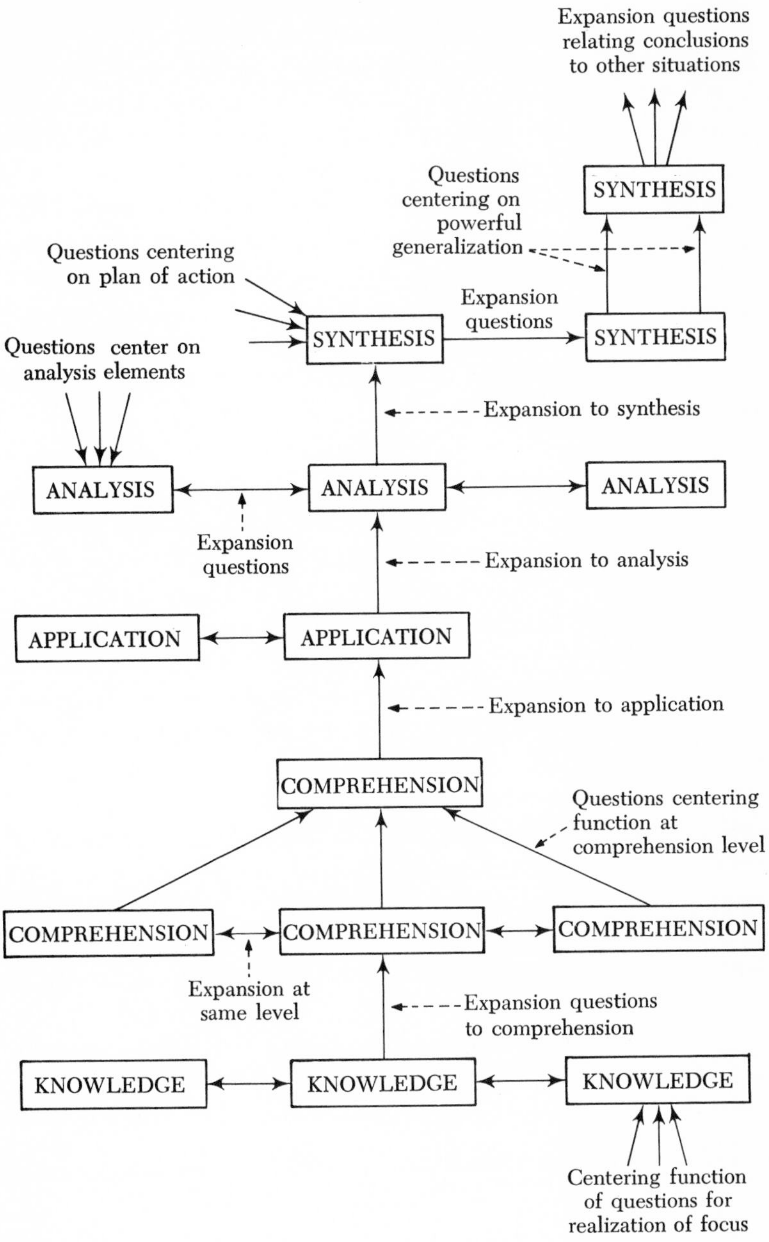

Figure 4.3. Questions using both centering and expansion functions

ending with "What does it mean?" The "what" questions can be loosely equated with the knowledge and perhaps the comprehension levels of Bloom. The "why" questions could be equated somewhat to the application and analysis levels. The "what-does-it-mean" questions could be likened to the synthesis and evaluation questions. However, the fit between Taba's questions and the levels of Bloom's taxonomy is somewhat risky for each of these levels of questions in Taba are asked at her three cognitive task levels. Therefore comparison should be considered with some degree of caution.

Taba advocated careful attention to both the planning and the use of questions in the class situation. Rather than posing questions at various levels to one or two pupils, she advocated that questions at one particular level be distributed to most, if not all, members of the class.[9] All of the "what" questions would be asked of all or most of the students. When most students had been afforded the opportunity to participate at this particular level, questions aimed at lifting the level of thought to a higher level would be used. In this case the second level of questioning, the "why" questions, would be used. Here again questions would be distributed to all or most class members. The questions would now function to extend thought at the same level. After satisfactory involvement at this level, questions would raise pupil cognitive activity to the "what-does-it-mean" stage. Again the teacher would attempt to involve the majority of the class.

Taba iterated that questions at a particular level had to be sufficient to involve even the slowest students. If not, such students would be lost in the interaction. Also, students not having the opportunity to participate at one particular plateau of questioning would lack the requisite understandings to effectively respond to higher levels of questions. Thus a student lost in the early parts of the inquiry or discovery session would be destined to fail or be nonproductive in later dealings with higher order questions.

[9] Ibid., pp. 123-25.

Taba also advocated complete involvement of students with questions at a particular step since she considered a premature raising of the thought to a higher level caused a decrease of student participation and a degeneration of total class thought to solely specific knowledge.[10] She stated that if adequate attention were provided to each level of questions before continuing to the next higher stage, the end product would represent high-level thought.

If we follow this particular strategy, we need to beware the temptation that once hearing a powerful student response to a particular question, we do not then ask a higher order question of that student and lead him from specific fact to generalization. However, many students may react negatively to the search for data if they are denied the opportunity to follow a particular train of thought to high-order abstractions. If they have to detain this search until most class members gather specifics, these students may be "turned off." However, we should experiment in our classrooms to ascertain how our students do react. Also, we need to remember that this is just one suggested questioning strategy.

Suchman's Inquiry Strategy

Suchman,[11] concerned about the lack of student involvement in their own learning, developed a strategy requiring active student participation. Here the teacher assumed the role of data source and guide.

In Suchman's strategy, students pose four types or classes of questions: verification, experimentation, necessity, and synthesis.[12] Verification questions are designed to obtain specific data to verify their existence. These are the fact-gathering

---

[10] Ibid., pp. 125-26.

[11] J. Richard Suchman, *The Elementary School Training Program in Scientific Inquiry*. U. S. Department of Health, Education, and Welfare, Office of Education, Cooperative Research Project no. 216. (Urbana, Ill.: University of Illinois, 1958), 129 pp.

[12] J. Richard Suchman, *Developing Inquiry* (Chicago: Science Research Associates, 1966), p. 56.

questions. Experimentation questions verbally manipulate information gathered at the verification level to determine the consequences of such manipulation. Necessity questions determine if particular data are essential for an event in question or under investigation to exist. Synthesis questions aim at ascertaining if ideas, hunches, or conclusions being considered as the result of prior questioning are valid or warranted. Suchman uses the term "theory" to identify the pupils' thinking when asking synthesis questions. It should be recognized that this is a loose interpretation of the term. Perhaps it is more accurate to consider such questions as attempts at testing hypotheses, intellectual hunches.

These four types of questions are asked about four types of data: events, objects, conditions, and properties.[13] *Events* refer to situations that happen or exist. Events can be problems comprising an investigation's focus. They can be last night's basic news story. They can be the experiments demonstrated in science class. *Objects* are elements existing as parts of the events. Suchman considered these as more abstract than events and existing within a time dimension. In a science experiment, objects can be the liquids used or the types of containers holding the substances. *Conditions* refer to the state of the objects. Conditions are alterable. If an experiment were being conducted with water, one might wish to know the condition— i.e., temperature—of the water. In investigating a person's behavior, the person's physical condition might be under scrutiny. *Properties* are unalterable characteristics. Properties of metal do not change and one can use these stable properties for metal identification. Gasoline has the property of being volatile. The metallic element mercury has the property of being liquid at room temperature. Oxygen has the properties of being a gas at room temperature and a liquid at 250 degrees below zero.

The prime differing aspect of Suchman's inquiry is that the teacher does not employ a questioning strategy. Rather,

---

[13] Ibid., pp. 56-57.

he allows students to employ a strategy. Strasser[14] has developed a listing of tactical moves which teachers can use to encourage students to question productively. The teacher's role is to provide a focus for the inquiry, allow students sufficient time to inquire, and to furnish support either verbally or through materials. This strategy of inquiry is one of guiding in the true sense: pupils are led to participate if they desire but no individual is forced to participate if he does not wish to at the particular time. Important to remember is that the teacher refrains from making decisions for the student. The student must assume responsibility for dealing with information and making his own decisions. Teachers encourage and assist the student's thinking, but the student must judge the worth, power, or validity of his investigation.

Questions Asked

As previously stated, Suchman suggests students can ask four types or classes of questions: verification, experimentation, necessity, and synthesis. The student can frame these questions in any sequence he wishes. For instance, he may commence his inquiry by asking verification questions attempting to gain an information base. He may then organize the results of this questioning and determine, through questioning, which data are necessary or crucial to his quest. He then might pose experimentation questions to conclude if the conditions, properties, or objects were necessary. By experimenting the student arranges information verbally: What would happen if I used this material instead of that? What might be the result if I took this person and employed him in this type of situation?

The teacher, functioning as a data source for students' questions, guides their investigations. For the students, the objective is to arrive via questioning at increased factual understanding, but more importantly, understanding of various concepts and generalizations. The teacher, as mentioned previously, has certain responses to guide the inquiry. If students

[14]Ben B. Strasser, *Components in a Teaching Strategy* (San Anselmo, Calif.: Search Models Unlimited, 1967), pp. 9-21.

pose verification questions or experimentation questions, the teacher can respond yes or no. To necessity or synthesis questions the teacher cannot provide such a response. Rather he must employ tactical moves to enable students to determine their own conclusions. More detail regarding these tactical moves can be found in Strasser's *Components in a Teaching Strategy*.[15]

Students asking verification or experimentation questions can receive either a yes or no response, or the teacher can provide data, theories, or names of objects. When students deal with synthesis and necessity questions, the teacher can probe for data and for various verbal processes that might be conducted. He also can provide some clues as to the most propitious operations or processes to use to gain data. If the teacher realizes students lack information to question further productively, he may decide to engage in instruction using some other teaching method.

Taba advocated major student involvement in asking questions at certain cognitive levels before the teacher posed questions that would raise the level of thought. With Suchman's method, a student who is questioning can have the floor until he has reached a standstill and then passes. Of course, if the student's questions are unproductive, the teacher might encourage him to pass and ponder further the particular situation. Once a student has passed, another student can engage in questioning starting with verification questions and proceed through the questioning types until he finally tests the feasibility of a theory or hypothesis.

If we were to diagram a flow of questions using Suchman's strategy, it might resemble Figure 4.4.

Figure 4.4 indicates a lesson dealing with water boiling at normal room temperature, 70 degrees. The first student began by asking several verification questions. These questions led him to formulate a necessity question, Was it crucial to use water in this situation? Rather than answering yes or no, the

---

[15] Ibid., pp. 1-47.

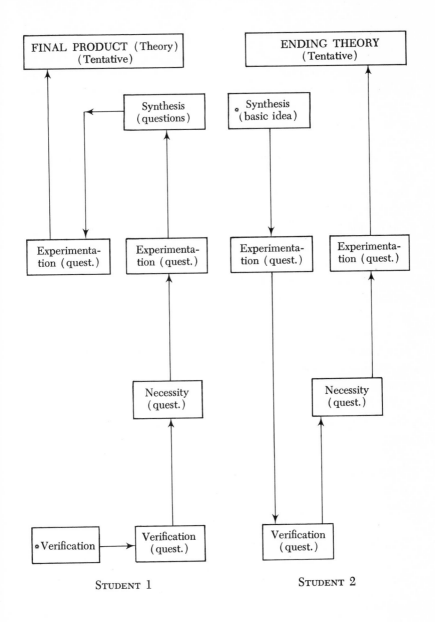

NOTE: * Indicates starting point for inquiry.

Figure 4.4. Diagrammed paths of students' inquiry

teacher asked the student how he might determine for himself if any other liquid could be used. Thus the student was led to ask experimentation questions. The student by means of questioning experimented with the object, which in this case was water. He might have asked questions about the effects on the event if another liquid had been used. He might have asked questions regarding the effects of altering the temperature of the water. The responses to these experimentation questions led the student to formulate a tentative idea or theory. However, the teacher may have asked the student to check further his thinking. Thus we see by the diagram that he engaged in further experimentation questions. He concluded his inquiry with a final tentative product—his theory. Notice that I have used "final" and "tentative." The product is final in that it ends this particular questioning sequence by the student; it is tentative in that the student may want to alter his basic idea as he confronts additional information.

The student now passes and student number two comes into the question sequence. Notice, by examining the directional flow of the arrows, that this second student begins his questioning by posing a basic idea or theory about the situation. Perhaps he is starting from where student number one ended. The teacher responds to his initial questions by asking him how he could test his ideas. What experimentation questions can he ask to gain needed information? The student follows the teacher's clue and engages in a series of experimentation questions. However, he discovers that he needs to pose some verification questions to further identify the several objects or events comprising the situation. Once the student has asked the verification questions, he then poses some necessity questions to determine relevant data. The teacher responds to the necessity questions by encouraging the student to engage in experimentation. The student does ask some experimentation questions and concludes with a statement which he accepts as a tentative theory. A third student could then participate in the inquiry or student number one could raise additional questions.

Not every student who formulates questions would ask all four types each time. Nor would he always proceed from verification or fact gathering to the abstract levels of forming hypotheses or generalizations. This diagram shows the strategies used by two hypothetical students in their attempt to gain understanding.

If inquiry were conducted with large numbers of students simultaneously, it is likely that one would lose many students as Taba has warned. However, this particular questioning strategy is optimally employed with small groups, usually about ten students. Thus most students have opportunities to participate. Also, in using inquiry I have found that students usually do not monopolize the question asking. If a student does monopolize a session, you can suggest that he allow other students to participate; in listening to their questions he may gain information of value to his search.

A Combination: Hunkins' Strategy

The questioning strategies implicit in Bloom's taxonomy and Suchman's inquiry have been presented. The next strategy we discuss is somewhat of a synthesis of these two. The initial level of students' questions depends largely on their readiness or background. If students have been engaged in a particular study for three weeks, it is unlikely that one would continue stressing knowledge.questions. Rather, following lessons might commence with analysis and synthesis questions. However, for discussion, let us assume that a group of students does not have a wealth of background experiences or information.

Thus the lesson begins with questions designed to elicit knowledge responses in order to lay a knowledge base with which students can work. It also allows the teacher to determine the knowledge level students possess and to anticipate potential difficulties. Questions at this knowledge level have a centering function. Students also would be encouraged to pose questions for investigation. When an adequate base of facts has been provided, comprehension questions are used in a strategy to raise student thought to a higher cognitive level. While working at the comprehension level, it may be necessary to drop back down the cognitive scale and pose questions at the knowledge level. Perhaps students were experiencing difficulty comprehending the author's meaning because of a lack of knowledge regarding specific terms. This first lesson might deal only with the knowledge and comprehension levels of questions.

The next lesson may have the objective of allowing students time to apply information they have gained either regarding process or information. Since application questions require time to engage various processes or principles, the questions this day are few in number. These questions focus on expansion of information to other situations. At the beginning of the lesson, application questions having the distribution function may be posed. The aim of such questions is to engage as many students as possible in the application stage. Perhaps the questions require the students to conduct diverse experiments. The students are scheduled reaction time. In this particular example, the teacher might move to different groups of students experiencing some difficulty at the application stage and pose questions at the comprehension and knowledge levels. They might also be encouraged to ask themselves questions at other levels. This strategy gradually raises the cognitive level of questions and discussion while allowing students to function at lower cognitive levels when additional information or rethinking is required.

Perhaps students are given two days for responding to the application stage. Results would be discussed and then students would be confronted with analysis questions. They might be given examples of some scientific phenomena in action. The students use questions to assist themselves in discovering significant elements of the situation and the relationships between the elements. At first the questions may comprise a strategy having a centering function in that certain elements are receiving focus. After these elements have been identified and defended as relevant, questions can assume an expansion function to encourage investigation at increased depth. Again, adequate time must be allowed for students to deal with these questions. Students are encouraged to ask questions at the lower levels of Bloom's Taxonomy when they need specific information or to reacquaint themselves with the main thesis of some author's discussion.

Following analysis, the next lesson would stress synthesis. Using this science lesson as our example, the questions would stress the development of a particular law to explain the phenomena under investigation. Next students could jointly compile data gathered in other lessons. Results of experiments would be presented. Elements deemed significant would be recorded and perhaps ranked. At first, the questions could have the centering function, attempting to get students to focus on one or two significant laws or principles that might explain the particular phenomena. Once the students had responded to this centering function, questions at the synthesis level geared to an expansion function would be asked. They would direct the students to consider other situations and ask them to explain these situations utilizing the law. If the phenomena under investigation had concerned the relationship between the attraction of matter and the size of the mass, then this principle might be applied to other situations.

After questions that expand the students' understanding on the level of synthesis have been asked, evaluation questions can be posed. Questions at this level could get students to apply criteria for determining the accuracy of a suggested law of science. Questions could ask the applicability of their findings. Again, these evaluation questions would have an initial centering function but then would shift to an expansion function. The teacher might ask questions at other levels of the taxonomy to clarify points or gain additional comprehension. New experiments might be needed to determine the applicability of conclusions to other situations. Students would be actively re-engaged in the application stage with appropriate questions being asked either by the teacher or by themselves.

In this strategy, questions have involved both the center-

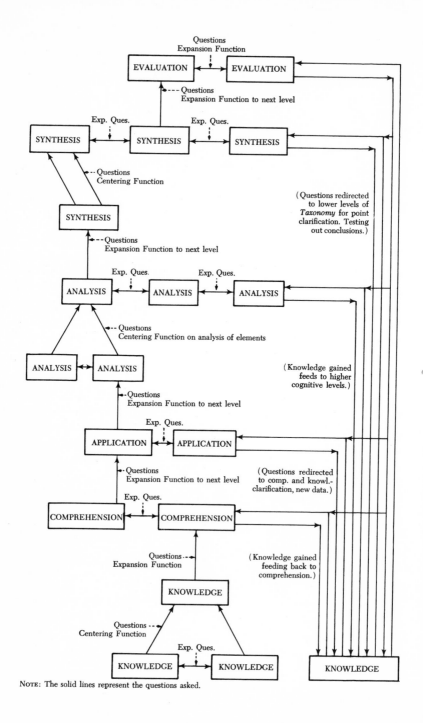

NOTE: The solid lines represent the questions asked.

ing and the expansion functions. However, the other two functions, distribution and order, also would have been used. At each level attempts would be made to involve most students in the activity. Students might be teamed together and distribute their questions among themselves. Relating to the order function, some questions would have a strictly management purpose, perhaps asking students if they knew the rules for working in the laboratory or for conducting a field study. Also, some questions would be aimed at providing students with support for their inquiries.

This lesson is diagrammed in Figure 4.5.

Not every lesson would be as complicated as this diagram suggests. If one were to begin at the analysis level, the questions primarily would be concerned with either centering or expansion of the analysis activities. Some questions might drop back to a lower level to gain specific facts or understandings. One would then have a scheme which would be represented by the top half of Figure 4.5.

Diagrams can enable one to study the particular questioning sequence used in a specific lesson. It is possible to construct such a diagram after a lesson has been completed. If the lesson sessions have been taped, one can record the questions asked, identify the level of thinking, and identify which questions expanded the cognitive level upward or which redirected students to lower cognitive levels. Such a diagram would be somewhat similar to the reaction avenues previously discussed.

Use of Supplementary Materials

Much attention has been given to the function of questions and questioning strategies. However, all questions, regardless of the strategy being used, are asked in relation to particular situations, contents, and materials. Today, there are many

---

Figure 4.5. (*facing*) Hunkins Combined Questioning Strategy

educational materials and projects from which to choose. It would be impossible to present even a sampling of all the projects in each area and how they can be considered from the questioning strategy standpoint. But, hopefully, the reader can apply the information presented in the first parts of this chapter to the projects or materials he is using in his class. Three types of educational materials will be considered.

Packaged Curricula

Curriculum packages can assist us in our teaching. Some of these packages incorporate different types of materials: primary source materials, artifacts, records, pictures, filmstrips, and booklets. Many of these packages organize the various materials to complement each other. Suggestions as to what questions to ask also are presented. Some projects include suggestions for ways of dealing with data and offer plans of attack. Implicit in these suggestions are questioning strategies. However, a difficulty is the diversity of the suggested means of working with the data. It would help if one could select from the questioning strategies mentioned in this chapter one that would involve students in learning regardless of the particular curriculum package. Certainly a specific questioning strategy is not realistic for each curriculum. I believe the Hunkins Combination Strategy introduced on page 101 is applicable to any of the new curricula regardless of the subject area.

We need to exercise caution not to accept blindly all the curriculum packages as including effective questions. Some projects in their objectives support the use of effective questions. Sometimes, however, this objective of involving students via questions is not really accomplished. Thus teachers should be sufficiently knowledgeable regarding questions to adapt those found in these projects to higher cognitive levels. We are going to have to plan our questioning strategies and not just accept those tentatively suggested in the materials.

In reviewing a new curriculum project for potential use,

we should analyze the questioning strategy implied. We should then determine how we must adjust or how we can effectively use our own questioning strategy with the materials. Four steps in dealing with such materials are: (1) analysis of the materials to identify the questioning strategy implied; (2) consideration of aspects that will need to be adapted to your particular questioning strategy and your particular class; (3) discussion of your questioning plan with a colleague to see if it has a power potential for getting students to achieve your objectives and the curriculum package's objectives; and (4) planning a trial of your questioning strategy with the materials to determine effectiveness.

Textbooks

Previous mention was made of questions in textbooks. Many textbooks fall short of having quality questions. When considering a particular questioning strategy, whether an overall strategy or a particular strategy for a certain lesson, we need to consider how or where to use the textbook. Are we going to use it when asking comprehension questions to center on a particular topic? Will we use the textbook as a jumping-off place and use primarily expansion questions at the comprehension level?

Once we have determined how we will use the textbook, we need to direct attention specifically to the questions included. Often we will have to upgrade the questions to emphasize higher cognitive levels. We need to be well acquainted with the questions in the textbook in order to incorporate these questions into our total questioning-teaching strategy.

Films and Filmstrips

An exciting new development in films is the film without the explanatory narration. In Bruner's *Study of Man*,[16] the film on

[16] Jerome Bruner, *Man, A Course of Study* (Cambridge, Mass.: Educational Development Center, 1968).

Eskimos shows them in their daily living. Other films on the market show certain tribes in Africa making boats, or growing and processing onions. These films, since they have no narration, allow us great freedom as to how we use them and what types of questions we can employ. We should certainly use these new materials in ways suitable to stimulate the higher cognitive levels. Again, we need to consider where we will use these new materials in the total questioning strategy. What are some questions we can use that stress analysis? What questions can we employ to expand the level of thought from analysis to synthesis? to expand the level of thought at the synthesis level?

Much of what we have said about films can be said for filmstrips. We should not use filmstrips just to stress knowledge or comprehension. Filmstrips can stimulate analysis questions. A student with a teammate can use filmstrips in investigating questions.

Regardless of what supplementary materials are selected, we still must plan a questioning strategy for our class. The materials can present the information or some of it; they can even suggest the processes to employ, but the specific questioning strategy is our challenge and our responsibility.

SUMMARY

This chapter began with a discussion of the functions of questioning strategies. Four functions were identified: two guiding functions, one strategy-management function, and one classroom-control function. The first guiding function, centering, was used primarily to direct students' attention to a particular investigation or to an aspect of the investigation. The expansion function was the second guiding function. Here the prime objective was to guide students' divergent thinking at the several cognitive levels. The distribution function was the strategy-management function. Here the aim was at involving students in working with data. The order function, the last function discussed, was aimed at maintaining a classroom atmosphere conducive to an effective discovery curriculum.

Next we considered questioning strategies including the strategy implicit in Bloom's Taxonomy, Taba's strategy, Suchman's inquiry strategy, and my combination strategy. Diagrams of these strategies were presented.

Last, attention was directed to the use of strategies with educational materials. This section briefly considered packaged curricula, textbooks, films, and filmstrips. Even though many of the current materials are excellent, there is need for carefully planning and developing questions to get students actively involved in the discovery curriculum.

5

Means of Evaluation

Questions are complex and require careful planning. But we also need to determine the success of our planning: Have we guided and facilitated student learning? Have our questions stimulated thought among students? Have our questions motivated them to action? Have our questions stimulated students' affective dimensions? Have we used the questions we had planned? Have our questions allowed students to respond at planned cognitive levels? Have we provided students with necessary supporting materials and allowed them enough time for adequate response? To answer such questions requires having means of evaluation. This chapter considers some means of obtaining feedback on our questions and question-asking behaviors as well as information on the questions and question-asking behaviors of our students. The feedback schema discussed are not the only ones available; they may trigger the reader into thinking of additional ones.

EXISTING SCHEMA

Numerous schema exist to provide us with information regarding the total teaching act. Most of us have heard of Ned

Flanders and his interaction analysis.[1] Flanders's scheme allows the teacher to obtain information in ten categories: (1) accepts feelings; (2) praises or encourages; (3) accepts or uses ideas of student; (4) asks questions; (5) lecturing; (6) giving directions; (7) criticizing or justifying authority; (8) student talk-response; (9) student talk-initiation, and (10) silence or confusion.

Only one segment deals with questions. His concern is whether the teacher asks questions about content or procedure in order to elicit a student response. For the teacher to obtain greater understanding of his questions, another type of feedback instrument must be used.

Another general system of obtaining feedback was developed by Herbert.[2] Herbert's observation instrument (Record of Lesson Observation—ROLO) also considers the total teaching act. It considers lesson form which deals with teaching strategies. It considers verbal and nonverbal communication in the classroom. It considers how students are encouraged to interact with the teacher and subject matter. Grouping and location techniques of the teacher also are outlined. Subject matter is examined in this scheme. Here focus is on the subjects the teacher is stressing. Herbert's scheme also directs attention to the form of the subject matter: Is the subject matter presented in depth study or in a comparison of functions of various societies? What is the sequence of subject topics? Herbert's observation schedule also diagnoses the techniques the teacher employs in managing his class. The ROLO also allows for the recording of the types of media used in a lesson but information specifically regarding the question is not provided.

[1] Ned A. Flanders, *Teacher Influence, Pupil Attitudes and Achievement: Studies in Interaction Analysis.* U. S. Department of Health, Education, and Welfare, Office of Education, Cooperative Research Project No. 397. (Minneapolis: University of Minnesota, 1960).

[2] John Herbert, *A System for Analyzing Lessons* (New York: Teachers College Press, Columbia, 1967).

Question Record Sheet—
Extended Suchman Matrix

Earlier we considered Suchman's inquiry strategy. Suchman developed a sheet on which to record the exact types of questions that, according to his system, students were asking. You recall that these question types were verification, experimentation, necessity, and synthesis. An example of such a question record sheet is presented in Table 5.1.

This sample deals with a lesson on urban sprawl. The teacher is attempting to guide students to discover the cause for urban sprawl in a particular region and also how the transportation system might alleviate some of the problems such sprawl has created. The question record sheet indicates the person asking questions and the type of questions posed. In the left-hand column are brief key words to remind the teacher of the question.

The student John begins the session by asking three verification questions relating to objects: How many cars? How many people? How many freeways? Mary then asks verification questions relating to events to see if the city had a master plan for its development and for its traffic. She queries who decided the master plan for the freeway's location. Her next question was a necessity question regarding the need for using cars. She then was directed by the teacher to experiment to determine this. She next asked a question experimenting (E_e) with various other means of transportation. Then Doreen raised a verification question of the event relating to people voting.

At the bottom of the page the total number of questions asked by each student is listed, and these totals are further divided into question types. From such a record sheet we can determine the extent and the cognitive level of student involvement. In looking at such a record sheet one should not expect a magical formula as to what is an effective lesson or an ideal sequence of questions. The effectiveness of this particular lesson can only be judged in light of the objectives that the teacher had planned. If this sample lesson's main focus had been to stimulate students to think about the problem of urban sprawl, then the lesson most likely would be judged effective.

You also recall that in Suchman's strategy, a child can ask as many questions as he desires and, hopefully, will ask increasingly complex or high-level questions. In this example, several instances were exhibited of this raising-of-question level. Mary asked two verification questions, then a necessity question, and then experimented. Doreen asked a verification question, then a necessity question, and then experimented to ascertain certain data. Doreen, in questions 15 through 18, posed questions indicating her dealing with data in order to derive a theory, an hypothesis, or a tentative conclusion. Her questions were not solely at the data-gathering level.

Such a question record also can indicate the individual pupil's approach to an inquiry session. John in this session was content, at least at first, to gather data. Mary, after a brief gathering of data, desired to experiment. Doreen was involved in gathering and then dealing with data. In looking at the record of Francis, question number 13 reveals that, even though he had not been asking any questions at the beginning of the session, he had been actively listening since when he did question, it was at the theory level. It further indicates his contentment with his theory, since he did not ask any experimentation questions to test his theory. The more one deals with this particular form of inquiry-discovery and uses a record sheet of this type, the more information one will be able to extract from it.

Strasser has developed what he calls an "Extended Suchman Matrix." It follows the same basic principles as the question record sheet, except that the teacher's tactical moves are recorded in addition to the students' quesions. This form allows the teacher to study a student's questions and his responses to them. Table 5.2 is an example of the Extended Suchman Matrix.

Table 5.1
Inquiry Development Question Record Sheet

Teacher_____ Time_____
Date_____
Film or Problem: URBAN SPRAWL
Session: 1   Page No._____

	Events	Objects	Conditions	Properties
Verification	V_e	V_o	V_c	V_p
Experimentation	E_e	E_o	E_c	E_p
Synthesis	S_e	S_o	S_c	S_p
Necessity	N_e	N_o	N_c	N_p

SPECIFIC QUESTIONS	JOHN	MARY	SAM	MAC	DOREEN	FRANCIS	LEAH				
1. No. of cars	V_o										
2. No. of people	V_o										
3. No. of freeways	V_o										
4. Master plan?		V_e									
5. Who decided?		V_e									
6. Necessity cars?		N_e									
7. Other trans?		E_e									
8. People voted?					V_e						
9. Peoples' wishes?					N_e						
10. Polled people?					E_e						
11. Where in city?			V_o								
12. Where prob. begin?			V_e								

13. Sprawl = landform?
14. Elevation site?
15. Necessary to solve?
16. Add air trans?
17. Add trains?
18. Various systems?
19.
20.
21.
22.
23.
24.
25.

				N_e E_e E_o S_e	S_e	V_e	
Total Questions	3	4	2	7	1	1	9
Verification	3	2	2	1		1	4
Experimentation		1		3	1		2
Synthesis		1		1			3
Necessity				2			

Totals

SOURCE: From *Developing Inquiry* by J. Richard Suchman. © 1966, Science Research Associates, Inc. Reproduced by permission of the publisher.

Table 5.2
Extended Suchman Matrix

	BARRY	DEBBIE	DAVID	JIM	BILLY	POLLY	JEAN	ROBERT
1.	Eo_1 $I3$ Eo_2 $I7$ Eo_3 $R3$							
2.		Vo R3						
3.			Ec R3–R4					
4.						No_1 $I9$ No_2 $R2–I3$ Eo_3 $R1$ Eo_4 $R3$ Eo_5 $R3–I4$ Eo_6		
5.					R3–I4 S R5			

SOURCE: Ben B. Strasser, *Components in a Teaching Strategy Tactical Moves in Inquiry*, Unit I (San Anselmo, Calif.: Search Models Unlimited, 1967), p. 28. Reprinted by permission.

The Extended Suchman Matrix codes effective units, which are single operations conducted by the student rather than particular questions. An effective unit can contain both student's question and teacher's response. For example, Barry asks three experimentation questions indicated Eo_1, Eo_2, and Eo_3. The Eo have the subscripts $_1$, $_2$, $_3$ to indicate that the E's are questions relating to the same operation. To these questions the teacher has responded I3, I7, and R3. Briefly, the I3 is a probe for specificity, the I7 is a probe for explanation, and the R3 is a response to the student's data probe.

Barry's E questions and the teacher's reaction to each comprise one effective unit. The number 1 to the left of the Matrix indicates this effective unit. Debbie next engages in asking a verification question about an object to which the teacher reacts with the tactical move of responding to the student's data probe. This student question and teacher response constitutes the second effective unit. The number 2 at the left of the Matrix indicates this unit. One can observe that effective unit number 4 involving Polly has several types of pupil questions and teacher responses.

The Extended Matrix provides more data than Suchman's Question Observation Record. The Matrix enables us not only to consider and evaluate the effectiveness of the student's questioning but to check how effectively we are teaching.

Taba Cognitive Maps

On pages 14 to 16 we considered Taba's concept of cognitive maps. Such maps can either be developed before the students engage in working with information or after a lesson, while listening to an audio tape of a class session or sessions. If one lists the questions and inserts them into the cognitive map, an idea as to the effectiveness of the questions can be derived. The example given on page 15 considers how water might affect the way of life in a desert. Questions were used to raise the level of thinking from specific data to interpretation of data to the application of principles. One could construct a cognitive map and, along with the content consideration, record on it the specific questions posed by the students or oneself. One could also code the cognitive level of the question.

Recording Ideal-Active Cognitive Levels

In Chapter 3 we discussed the ideal and actual cognitive levels of questions. The ideal emphasis represented a question's highest implied cognitive level. It was the level that would be in effect if all the variables were optimal, such as student's ability, background, necessary support materials, adequate time, and powerful motivation. The actual level indicated the cognitive level of a student's response to the question. It was mentioned that the actual level really could not be determined until after the lesson had been conducted. Sometimes the response of the student is to ask another question. After a lesson is completed, one could develop a schematic such as the following:

IDEAL	ACTUAL	AGREEMENT
T 1. What is existentialism? (*knowledge terminology*)	S A philosophy based on the belief in the sole existence of man. (*knowledge*)	+
T 2. What is the author's central assumption regarding man's existence? (*analysis of elements*)	S Another philosopher stated that our author considered man as being alone entirely. (*comprehension —interpretation*)	−
T 3. What can be said regarding how we should structure the school situation in light of the existentialist view? (*synthesis— formation of a generalization*)	S An existentialist school environment would foster an awakening of the self to responsible self-action. (*formation of generalization*)	+

IDEAL	ACTUAL	AGREEMENT
S	T	
4. How might this relate to art? (*synthesis*)	Would another student like to reply?	(0)

KEY:
T = Teacher   + = agreement
S = Student   − = disagreement

Notice the teacher initiated the first three questions and the student reasoned in the actual realm. Agreement or non-agreement is indicated on the chart. However, after question 3 was phrased, a student asked a synthesis question. Thus this question was placed in the "Ideal" column. Such a question could not have been planned and would not have appeared in the Ideal column initially. Also, note that the teacher, instead of responding to the question, redirected the question to the other members of the class. Thus the teacher's question has the function of distribution (management). For this reason, the "Agreement" column lists a zero to indicate that agreement is not possible since the question of the teacher is not really in reply to the student's question. The student who does respond to question 4 would have his response checked for agreement between ideal and actual cognitive levels.

Recording questions in this way provides a list of all questions asked by both teacher and students, the responses elicited, and whether the responses are at the cognitive levels desired. The effectiveness of questioning is indicated by the number of minuses and pluses. If the teacher has all pluses, then he is effective at least from the standpoint of having his questions do what had been intended. Students also could judge their questions with this scheme.

Criteria relating to what is effective questioning include several factors: the objectives of the lesson, the specific questions asked, the degree of student involvement, and the types of student questions, as well as the tentative understandings for that particular lesson. We need to constantly address ourselves to these points. How do my questions relate to my objectives? Do my questions trigger in students the thought levels desired? How effective are my questions in relation to student involvement? Have my questions enabled most if not all students to develop some of the understandings and behaviors planned? Also, we need to remember that students can plan objectives, and we need to analyze our questions and students' questions from the point of view of their objectives.

Teacher-Pupil Question Inventory

The use of the Ideal-Actual-Agreement scheme requires that questions and their responses be recorded. At times this may be too cumbersome for the teacher. The Teacher-Pupil Question Inventory, designed for analyzing teachers' questions and responses to them as well as pupils' questions and teacher responses, was developed by Davis and Tinsley[3] in 1967. Their system, which is easy to use, was developed for researching the types of questions that social studies student teachers asked in their classes. It includes nine categories: memory, interpretation, translation, application, analysis, synthesis, evaluation, affectivity, and procedure. Bloom's categories are evident, and there are two additional categories, affectivity and procedure. The affectivity dimension deals with questions directed to feelings, or appraisal. This level relates to the affective domain. The procedure level category deals with questions asked for classroom management reasons.

The TPQI requires observation for thirty minutes of five-minute divisions. Questions asked by either the teacher or a pupil are recorded by a number representing one of the nine categories. For coding the question, the intent as well as the question's wording serves to identify its cognitive level.

---

[3] Davis and Tinsley, op. cit.

Clegg[4] the same year used the TPQI to study the types of questions asked by six student teachers. Clegg modified the TPQI to have only six levels, each representing a level in Bloom: memory, comprehension, application, analysis, synthesis, and evaluation. A copy of this version of the Teacher-Pupil Question Inventory follows:

TEACHER-PUPIL QUESTION INVENTORY

Teacher_____Data Observed_____

Grade_____

Lesson Objective_____

1. Memory
2. Comprehension
3. Application

4. Analysis
5. Synthesis
6. Evaluation

Indicate the level of question by using a number of the appropriate Bloom cognitive category.

First Five Minutes

Teacher's Questions	Q	
	R	
Pupils' Questions	Q	
	R	

Second Five Minutes

Teacher's Questions	Q	
	R	
Pupils' Questions	Q	
	R	

[4] Ambrose A. Clegg, Jr., George T. Farley, and Robert U. Curran, *Training Teachers to Analyze the Cognitive Level of Classroom Questioning.* University of Massachusetts, School of Education, Applied Research Training Program, Research Report No. 1. (Amherst, Mass.: University of Massachusetts, 1967).

Third Five Minutes

Teacher's Questions	Q	
	R	
Pupils' Questions	Q	
	R	

Fourth Five Minutes

Teacher's Questions	Q	
	R	
Pupils' Questions	Q	
	R	

Fifth Five Minutes

Teacher's Questions	Q	
	R	
Pupils' Questions	Q	
	R	

Sixth Five Minutes

Teacher's Questions	Q	
	R	
Pupils' Questions	Q	
	R	

NOTE: This TPQI Inventory is an adaptation of both the Davis and Tinsley form and the Clegg form.

SOURCE: O. L. Davis, Jr. and Drew C. Tinsley, "Cognitive Objectives Revealed by Classroom Questions Asked by Social Studies Student Teachers," *Peabody Journal of Education*, XLV, no. 1, July 1967, pp. 21-16. Reprinted by permission.

The TPQI's appealing aspect is its ease of use. The most difficult part is becoming familiar with the various types of questions as coded by Bloom. Whenever a question is asked or a response is given, the teacher records the action. In the Clegg version, the responses are coded 1 through 6: 1 for knowledge or memory, 2 for comprehension, 3 for application, 4 for analysis, 5 for synthesis, and 6 for evaluation. This recording would be done by listening to a tape of a lesson or a colleague could come in and code the questions during a lesson. Following is an example and discussion of ten minutes of a lesson:

TEACHER-PUPIL QUESTION INVENTORY

Teacher_____Data Observed_____

Grade_____

Lesson Objective_____

1. Memory	4. Analysis
2. Comprehension	5. Synthesis
3. Application	6. Evaluation

Indicate the level of question by using a number of the appropriate Bloom cognitive category.

First Five Minutes

Teacher's Questions	Q	1 1 2		2 2 3		2
	R		1 1		3	
Pupils' Questions	Q		1 1			
	R	1 1 1		2 2	3	

Second Five Minutes

Teacher's Questions	Q	4		5	
	R				
Pupils' Questions	Q				
	R		4		5

The teacher starts by asking a knowledge question. A pupil responds at the knowledge level. This response is indicated by a 1 placed in the R row in the pupils' question section. The teacher poses another knowledge question, which is followed by a pupil knowledge response. The teacher then formulates a comprehension question that is responded to at the knowledge level. Perhaps the student only recalled a response a classmate had made regarding a similar question. The pupil then poses a knowledge question, indicated by a 1 in the Q row in the pupils' question section. This is the fourth question asked in the lesson. The teacher responds at the knowledge level, perhaps supplying some data requested. The pupil interacts with another knowledge question, reacted to by the teacher at the same level. Perhaps this pupil needed some specific data before continuing productivity. Notice that the questions then go to comprehension and in the middle of the five minutes, the teacher poses an application question.

We have some spaces in our five-minute period. Such pauses indicate time required to respond to an application question. Toward the end of the first five minutes, the student or students respond to the application question with an application response. Such a response indicates students have processed information in reply to the question posed. Instead of phrasing another question, the teacher reacts to the pupil's response. Then a comprehension question is phrased, ending the first five-minute segment.

The second five-minute segment begins with an analysis question. Notice that a response to that question did not occur until about two and one-half minutes had elapsed. The time lapse indicates time required for reaction. When the pupil response did occur, it was at the same cognitive level. The teacher then asked synthesis questions. Perhaps the teacher wished the student or students to consider information gained at the analysis level and synthesize it into some type of statement having general applicability. In the last part of the second five minutes, the students responded with some type of generalization, which was recorded as a 5 response.

This example represents the way a questioning session could develop. It is possible that when dealing with higher-level questions, some of the five-minute segments would lack any marks because the students would not be responding verbally but would be investigating. The level of that investigation can only be determined with this type of scheme when the students actually respond verbally.

What does the TPQI tell us? First, it informs us of the kind and number of questions we asked in a thirty-minute period. It also reveals whether questions designed to stimulate certain stages of cognitive functioning are actually doing so. It indicates whether pupils are asking any questions or are just responding to our questions. Is such information good? Does it tell us whether we are asking effective questions or employing questions in a meaningful strategy? Again, the effectiveness of the questions phrased can only be judged in relation to the objectives planned for the particular lesson. If we desired students to gain a knowledge of specifics and to comprehend some information in certain class materials, the first five minutes would indicate success in achieving that goal. However, if we also had the objective of allowing students to phrase the majority of the questions, then we failed to achieve that aim.

In the same lesson, the teacher in the second five minutes posed analysis and synthesis questions and allowed students opportunity to deal with these questions. That students were able to deal with these questions, evidenced by their responses at the same cognitive level, indicates success. One thing to bear in mind is that while students were responding to the analysis questions in the second five-minute segment, they also may have been asking themselves questions which they did not verbalize to the total class. These questions, of course, cannot be recorded on the TPQI. To indicate the existence of such questioning, students can record their inquiry-behavior on their own TPQI. They would probably need to tape a group session to obtain such information.

The TPQI can indicate the particular questioning strategy being employed. The sample lesson indicates that during the first ten minutes of the lesson, the teacher used a strategy of raising the level of students' functioning to increasingly higher levels. In the third five-minute segment, not shown, the teacher might have allowed the students to deal with questions below the level of analysis and synthesis in order to pick up additional data or to phrase questions directing them to alternate avenues of investigation. If so, the questioning strategy would resemble the Hunkins Combination Strategy considered in the preceding chapter.

The TPQI does not indicate which pupil is responding or asking the questions. This information could be supplied if one had code numbers for each student and used each code as a subscript below the number representing a question's or response's particular cognitive level. Thus the student Doreen might have the code number 3. If Doreen had responded to an analysis question at the analysis level, then it could be recorded on the TPQI as 4_3. Such subscripting would indicate not only the level of pupil thinking but exactly who is responding.

The Teacher-Pupil Question Inventory records questions asked and their sequencing. Increased familiarity with this instrument allows one to experiment with various uses, e.g. subscripting numbers to indicate particular pupil involvement, or using it to gain insight into questions and questioning strategies. We in education need to record our actions and analyze results against intentions. The TPQI seems an optimal instrument for providing us with data regarding our questioning competence and the degree to which we are allowing pupils to participate in the discovery curriculum.

THE NEED FOR STUDENTS TO OBTAIN FEEDBACK

Few would contest the importance of teacher feedback. Yet we often overlook the fact that if students are to be productive in dealing with discovery curriculum, they also require opportunities and means of obtaining feedback. No reason exists to prevent students from being trained to use such devices as Suchman's Question Record Sheet and the Teacher-Pupil Question Inventory. If students are to become competent in questioning, they need information regarding the effectiveness of their question-asking. It is important that they engage in self-analysis. The teacher as sole evaluator tends to exclude the partnership approach to students' learning in which the teacher plays a guiding role. Also, a crucial aspect of learning includes acquiring the skills of self-analysis. Helping students to understand and use instruments such as the TPQI would be part of the formal and informal instruction on questions previously advocated. Certainly, a selling point for student use of the TPQI is its simplicity.

MINI-TEACHING FOR IMPROVING QUESTIONS AND QUESTIONING STRATEGIES

In attending to question improvement, we may wish to conduct a few mini-teaching situations. Some might consider mini-teaching identical to micro-teaching. However, I am using the term "mini-teaching" for teaching geared to an overall lesson or unit in the regular classroom. Also, instead of reteaching the same lesson as done in micro-teaching, the teacher, after analyzing his particular performance in a mini-lesson, would go on to a new aspect of the lesson or unit but attempt to initiate the same type questions or questioning strategy.

Information presented in the previous sections and chapters can be used in a mini-teaching situation. The writing of reaction avenues can be incorporated and taught in a mini-lesson. The stress would be on the types of questions used to focus and expand students' attention on selected topics. The lesson might then be analyzed for teacher's response to pupils' reactions and for questions used in advancing the lesson toward particular objectives.

In planning a mini-lesson, attention would center on the specific development of questions. Colleagues can assist here in judging tentatively planned questions. The material on cognitive maps and reaction avenues can be considered. The mini-lesson might aim at developing a focus. A lesson can be recorded on video tape. After ten minutes, the tape is analyzed to see how successfully the focus setting questions were used. Did the students become excited about the topic? Did the focusing questions draw upon students' prior background? What were the types of questions used in setting the focus? What degree of student participation existed in the focus setting activity? Were students allowed to offer additional foci for possible investigation?

It is optional as to what forms one uses in recording both teacher and student performance. Several have been mentioned in this textbook. If one is mini-teaching to improve the level of agreement between questions' ideal intended cognitive level and questions' actual level in class use, the format suggested on pages 118–19 might be productive.

Ideal	Actual	Agreement
1. (T) question	(P) question response	+ or −
2. (T) question	(P) question response	+ or −
3. (P) question	(T) response	+ or −

Key: T represents teacher; P represents pupil.

Since all questions can comprise strategies having various functions, one could teach a mini-lesson utilizing a strategy emphasizing one function at a particular cognitive level. One could study the parallel functions of distribution and order to determine types of relationships that may exist between the guiding function of expansion and the maintenance functions of distribution and order. Again, the teacher can develop a form to record such data. Such a form might resemble the following:

		Functions		
Questions	Cognitive Level	Expansion	Distribution	Order
1	analysis	yes	yes	
2	analysis	yes	yes	
3	analysis	yes		yes

The increasing use of video tape in schools allows us opportunity for self-analysis. We can not only use it to teach students but to experiment with the different methods, in this case questioning strategies, that we utilize to make learning meaningful.

The overall mini-teaching schedule can mirror that of micro-teaching. One can teach a mini-lesson and then, while a colleague takes over the class, analyze the lesson. This can then be repeated, perhaps emphasizing a different aspect of the same lesson to try out a new approach, or to practice again a particular strategy. However, the teach-analyze-reteach cycle need not be done within the same hour. Indeed, the analysis may not take place until a free period or the end of the day, and the reteaching may not take place until the next day.

In engaging in this mini-teaching, we are not only improving our questioning, we are assuming a new and challenging role, that of the educational investigator. No longer do we just try to teach and wait for others to come along and tell us how to improve our teaching. We are engaged in a continual analysis of our own teaching to gain increased understanding of the teaching act, particularly the questioning act. We are engaged in improving our fund of professional knowledge. We are assuming many of the characteristics of the autonomous learner that we stress for our students.

This discussion has far-reaching implications for us. The term "teacher" is currently assuming new meaning. The teacher's role is no longer that of the dispenser of knowledge. What specific new roles the educator will assume in the next decade are still to be discovered. However, teachers must be willing to question present roles and to seek new roles in order to feel comfortable in the latter part of this decade. These evolving roles need to be considered carefully if the promise of the discovery curriculum is to be fulfilled.

Summary

This chapter focused on means of feedback—self-evaluation and student evaluation. Some self-diagnostic schema for analyzing classroom phenomena were discussed. The Extended Suchman Matrix and the Question Record Sheet were presented in some detail. The evaluation of ideal-actual cognitive emphasis of questions also received attention.

Major focus was given to the Teacher-Pupil Question Inventory as a means for obtaining insight into questions. This scheme was cited for its ease of application and· the numerous types of information that can be derived from it. Attention was given to the need for allowing students opportunities to obtain feedback regarding their questions in order for them to become self-functioning in the discovery curriculum.

Mini-teaching in order to improve one's questions and questioning strategies and forms one can use to analyze tapes were considered.

This discussion implies our assuming new roles. We need to investigate the educative process as well as to teach students. We must accept the future's challenge for the discovery curriculum.

6

On Using
the Strategies

The questions and strategies discussed in this textbook are appropriate for all levels of education. Perhaps you are a primary or intermediate teacher and consider the discussion applicable only to the secondary teacher. Perhaps you at the elementary level think that following such questioning strategies will cause you to neglect the basic skills. Or perhaps you feel one should provide pupils with base information to be used later at the secondary level when more depth is required. Perhaps you as a secondary teacher feel the strategies appropriate for your students but not feasible to follow, since the time involved in using them would be unrealistically lengthy. How will I get through the text on American history? How will I present the required material in chemistry if I schedule too much time for students to ask questions? if I spend too much time asking questions just relating to one or two concepts? Surely this kind of question-asking demands more time than is available in the present school schedule.

This book is directed to all teachers, grades K through college level. The question incorporated into effective questioning strategies should exist at all levels of education. The types of questions discussed can be asked in grade one or in the senior year of college. Children of primary-school age are not too young to deal with each of the levels of questions. Of course, the degree of sophistication at each cognitive level will be adjusted to the pupils' intellectual maturity level. But children in the first grade can analyze what is happening in their world; they can formulate some general statements about their world; they can evaluate what is happening in their world. This also can be done at the college level. Students' answers will be more sophisticated but they will be similar in kind.

Planning for effective questions is basically the same regardless of the level of education. The same strategies can be used at all levels. I have used the Suchman strategy, the Taba strategy, and my combination questioning strategy at all levels of education—primary, intermediate, secondary, and college. Certainly student responses varied at each level. The amount of background information varied; the amount of guidance required varied. In a first-grade class I conducted a Suchman inquiry session. The children, as is often the case, had numerous ideas of why the particular event had happened. I had to spend some time guiding them in gathering specific facts to support their ideas. In a college level class I conducted a lesson which had the same focus. The students first gathered specific facts before advancing an idea to explain the focus. Students at this level did not need to amass large amounts of specific data. They generalized sooner because individuals at the college level already have large stores of information which they can bring to bear on their inquiry.

The emphasis one places on the components of the strategies can vary from one grade level to another but the strategies remain basically the same. In dealing with the Hunkins Combination Strategy in grade 4, one might spend more time asking knowledge and comprehension questions and getting pupils to ask such questions than in a grade 12 class. Hopefully, the majority of the questions in grade 12 would be at the levels of analysis, synthesis, and evaluation. This does not exclude questions being asked at the other levels. But the time spent with questions directed at specifics or just comprehending materials read or heard is likely to be less at the higher levels.

However, who is asking most of the questions should vary with the levels. At the elementary levels, the teacher asks most of the questions. Later, as they progress through the grades, pupils should assume greater questioning roles. While students will learn from viewing the teacher as an effective questioner, they probably need some formal lessons focused on just what the question is, how to employ questions as handles for grasping new information, and how to use questions as guides in independent investigation. Again, this focusing on questions can be done at all levels of education. Of course, the manner of presentation and student involvement will vary with the age and grade level. But students need to know that the question can be used to assist them in finding and relating information. Further, they can discover that certain types of questions are more likely to provide them with certain kinds of information than other types of questions. For example, if they wish to detect significant ideas in a story, they can ask questions either at the level of comprehension or analysis. If they pose only knowledge questions about facts presented, they will not be able to determine the author's significant ideas, unless the author has specifically mentioned that such and such is important for the reader to remember. As students augment their understanding of the question and questioning strategies, they will be able to assume greater responsibility for their learning.

EFFECTS OF QUESTIONING STRATEGIES
ON TEACHING BEHAVIOR

When we read books dealing with teaching strategies, we may react with interest but discount much of what is presented because it requires a dramatic change in our mode of functioning. If we accept the goal of process learning—of getting students involved in their learning—then we must be willing to change our methods. If we continually react to what is new by saying it cannot be done in our present situation, then little progress can be expected. In order to use these several questioning strategies we may have to adjust our educational goals. We may have to adjust our relationships to our students. We will have to avoid overstressing facts and striving to give everyone the same factual knowledge. We can guide students in obtaining a common understanding of some concept or generalization without involving all of them with the same content or in the same activity. The concept of freedom can be developed in the study of history or sociology or anthropology. The concept of population dynamics can be developed in social studies or in science. It can even be developed when dealing with certain mathematical models. However, the questions we ask need to be a part of some strategy.

If pupils are to gain expertise in their own questioning strategies, we cannot be so concerned with coverage that we hang on to the sole use of the method of exposition. We need to balance exposition with periods in which the students are the major question-askers and the major planners of their learning. Certainly this places demands on the time schedule. Periods may have to be extended beyond the regular forty to forty-five minutes. Are we willing to adjust the schedule? We need to continue to push for this flexibility as well as to be flexible outside of the regular school day and building.

In addition to adjusting the time schedule, we need to consider what these questioning strategies imply regarding the structure of the learning environment. We may want to turn our classrooms into laboratories. We can organize classrooms that allow simulated activities. We can take our students into the surrounding community more often to engage them in asking questions effectively. If we wish students to formulate questions at the level of analysis, the most productive learning environment may be the corner block in town rather than the classroom. If we accept the idea of students becoming the major questioners in their learning process, are we also willing to accept the idea of getting the students out of the school building for more of their learning?

An Attitude for Teachers and Students

We need more precise understanding regarding the question and question-asking; I hope this text will make you more knowledgeable. But my goal for you is not solely to comprehend what I have written. I hope you are moved to some type of commitment and action. I hope you have begun to recognize more fully that questions are crucial to education from both the student's and the teacher's view. If you comprehend the types of questions and the several strategies after reading this text, then I am partially successful. However, I will not be totally successful until you are not only a thinker about questions but an asker of effective questions and a motivator of students' questioning behavior. Certainly commitment to action is requisite on our parts if students are to command their full potentials. The ability to ask effective questions is necessary for quality teaching that will enable students to participate fully in this world.

APPENDIX
Research Studies

This appendix lists some major research studies dealing with questions and questioning techniques. The research cited is divided into two major categories: questions and questioning, and questions in text-type materials.

Questions and Questioning

Adams, Thomas Howard. "The Development of a Method for Analysis of Questions Asked by Teachers in Classroom Discourse" (doctoral thesis, Rutgers, The State University, 1964).

Boone, Stanley M. "An Investigation of the Effect of Higher Level Questions on Reading Comprehension" (doctoral thesis, University of Washington, 1971).

Buggey, Lesley Joanne. "A Study of the Relationship of Classroom Questions and Social Studies Achievement of Second Grade Children" (doctoral thesis, University of Washington, 1971).

Clegg, Ambrose A., Jr., Farley, G. T., and Curran, R. J. "Training Teachers to Analyze the Cognitive Level of Classroom Questioning." Research Report No. 1, Applied Research Training Program, University of Massachusetts, 1967.

Crump, Claudia. "Self-Instruction in the Art of Questioning in Intermediate-Grade Social Studies" (doctoral thesis, Indiana University, 1969).

Davis, O. L., Jr., and Tinsley, D. C. "Cognitive Objectives Revealed by Classroom Questions Asked by Social Studies Student Teachers," *Peabody Journal of Education* 45 (1967):21–26.

Douce, Hermon L. "Raising the Cognitive Level of Teacher Questioning Behavior in Selected Schools" (doctoral thesis, University of Washington, 1971).

Floyd, William D. "An Analysis of the Oral Questioning Activity in Select Colorado Primary Classrooms" (doctoral thesis, Colorado State College, 1960).

Gatto, Frank M. "Pupils' Questions: Their Nature and Their Relationship to the Study Process" (doctoral thesis, University of Pittsburgh, 1929).

Haynes, Hubert C. "Relation of Teacher Intelligence, Teacher Experience, and Type of School to Types of Questions" (doctoral thesis, George Peabody College for Teachers, 1935).

Howard, R. G. "The Pre-Service Development of Teacher Skill in Reading Questioning Strategy" (doctoral thesis, Ball State University, 1970).

Hunkins, Francis P. "The Influence of Analysis and Evaluation Questions on Achievement and Critical Thinking in Sixth Grade Social Studies," U. S. Department of Health, Education, and Welfare, Final Report, Cooperative Research Project, 1968.

————. "The Influence of Analysis and Evaluation Questions on Achievement in Sixth Grade Social Studies," *Educational Leadership* (Research Supplement) January 1968.

————. "The Effects of Analysis and Evaluation Questions on Various Levels of Achievement," *Journal of Experimental Education* 38 (Winter 1969):45–58.

————. "Analysis and Evaluation Questions: Their Effects Upon Critical Thinking," *Educational Leadership* (Research Supplement) April 1970.

Manson, G. A. "The Effects of Immediate and Postponed Observer Feedback on the Acquisition of Higher Order Questioning Skills by Prospective Teachers" (doctoral thesis, University of Washington, 1970).

Moyer, J. R. "An Exploratory Study of Questioning in the Instructional Processes in Selected Elementary Schools" (doctoral thesis, Columbia University, 1966).

Quiring, Julia D. "The Effects of Questioning Level and Feedback Timing on the Achievement of Sophomore Nursing Students

Using an Auto-Tutorial Approach" (doctoral thesis, University of Washington, 1971).

Rogers, Virginia M. "Varying the Cognitive Levels of Classroom Questions in Elementary Social Studies: An Analysis of the Use of Questions by Student Teachers" (doctoral thesis, University of Texas, 1969).

Savage, Thomas V. "The Relationship of Classroom Questioning and Social Studies Achievement of Fifth Grade Students" (unpublished paper, University of Washington, 1971).

Schreiber, J. E. "Teacher's Question-Asking Techniques in Social Studies" (doctoral thesis, University of Iowa, 1967).

Stevens, Romiett. "The Question as a Measure of Efficiency in Instruction" (doctoral thesis, Columbia University, 1912).

Tinsley, Drew C. "A Study in Planning: Questions to Guide Discussion and Testing by Secondary Student Teachers of Social Studies" (doctoral thesis, University of Texas, 1968).

Tyler, June F. "A Study of the Relationship of Two Methods of Questioning Presentation, Sex and School Location to the Social Studies Achievement of Second-Grade Children" (doctoral thesis, University of Washington, 1971).

Yamada, Soshichi. "A Study of Questioning," *Pedagogical Seminary* 20 (1913):129–86.

Zoch, F. R. "The Effect of an Individualized In-Service Program on Teacher Questioning and Student Verbal Participation" (doctoral thesis, University of Houston, 1970).

Questions in Text-Type Materials

Davis, O. L., Jr., and Hunkins, Francis P. "Textbook Questions: What Thinking Processes Do They Foster?" *Peabody Journal of Education* 43 (March 1966):285–92.

Frase, L. T. "Effective Prose Reading: Shaping and Discriminative Effects of Questions." Paper read at the Annual Convention of the American Educational Research Association, Chicago, February 1968.

————. "Learning From Prose Material: Length of Passage, Knowledge of Results and Position of Questions," *Journal of Educational Psychology* 58 (1967):266–72.

Goldern, Sister Mary Laurentia. "Reading Guided by Questions Versus Careful Reading Followed by Questions," *Journal of Educational Psychology* 33 (September 1942):463–68.

Hearn, Delmer D. "Cognitive Operations Fostered by Questions in the Narrative and Captions of the Texas State-Adopted Geography Textbooks for Grade Six, 1966–67" (master's thesis, University of Texas, 1967).

Johnson, Harry W. "Certain Aspects of Guided Study-Type Reading by an Organized Pattern of Questions" (doctoral thesis, University of Chicago, 1951).

Natkin, G. and Stahler, E. "The Effects of Adjunct Questions on Short- and Long-term Recall of Prose Materials," *American Educational Research Journal* 6 (May 1969):425–32.

Rothkopf, E. A. and Bisbicos, E. E. "Selective Facilitative Effects of Interspersed Questions on Learning From Written Materials," *Journal of Educational Psychology* 58 (1967):56–61.

Washburne, John N. "The Use of Questions in Social Science Material," *The Journal of Educational Psychology* 22 (1929): 321–59.

Index